TOWARD A MARKET-ORIENTED HOUSING SECTOR IN EASTERN EUROPE

Developments in Bulgaria, Czechoslovakia, Hungary, Poland, Romania, and Yugoslavia

URBAN INSTITUTE REPORT 90–10

Jeffrey P. Telgarsky and Raymond J. Struyk

THE URBAN INSTITUTE PRESS

Washington, D.C.

THE URBAN INSTITUTE PRESS
2100 M Street, N.W.
Washington, D.C. 20037

Library of Congress Cataloging in Publication Data
Toward a Market-Oriented Housing Sector in Eastern Europe: Developments in Bulgaria, Czechoslovakia, Hungary, Poland, Romania, and Yugoslavia / Jeffrey P. Telgarsky and Raymond J. Struyk

1. Housing--Europe, Eastern. 2. Housing policy--Europe, Eastern. I. Struyk, Raymond J. II. Title. III. Series.

HD7332.9.T45	1990	90-49256
363.5'0947--dc20		CIP

(Urban Institute Reports; 90-10 ISSN 0897-7399)

ISBN 0-87766-496-X
ISBN 0-87766-495-1 (casebound)

Printed in the United States of America.

Distributed by University Press of America

4720 Boston Way	3 Henrietta Street
Lanham, MD 20706	London WC2E 8LU ENGLAND

URBAN INSTITUTE REPORTS are designed to provide rapid dissemination of research and policy findings. Each report contains timely information and in rigorously reviewed to uphold the highest standards of policy research and analysis.

The Urban Institute is a nonprofit policy research and educational organization established in Washington, D.C., in 1968. Its staff investigates the social and economic problems confronting the nation and government policies and programs designed to alleviate such problems. The Institute disseminates significant findings of its research through the publications program of its Press. The Institute has two goals for work in each of its research areas: to help shape thinking about societal problems and efforts to solve them, and to improve government decisions and performance by providing better information and analytic tools.

Through work that ranges from broad conceptual studies to administrative and technical assistance, Institute researchers contribute to the stock of knowledge available to public officials and private individuals and groups concerned with formulating and implementing more efficient and effective government policy.

Conclusions or opinions expressed in Institute publications are those of the authors and do not necessarily reflect the views of other staff members, officers or trustees of the Institute, advisory groups, or any organizations that provide financial support to the Institute.

ACKNOWLEDGMENTS

This Report draws heavily on five papers previously produced in 1990 by Urban Institute staff under contract to the Office of Housing and Urban Programs, U.S. Agency for International Development:

Transformation of the Housing Sector in Poland and Hungary, by Pamela Hussey, Jeffrey Telgarsky, Raymond Struyk, and Royce LaNier.

Yugoslavia: Background Notes on the Housing Sector in a Reforming Economy, by William Barnes and Jeffrey Telgarsky.

Romania: Background Notes on the Housing Sector in a Reforming Economy, by William Barnes and Jeffrey Telgarsky.

Czechoslovakia: Background Notes on the Housing Sector in a Reforming Economy, by William Barnes and Jeffrey Telgarsky.

Bulgaria: Background Notes on the Housing Sector in a Reforming Economy, by William Barnes, Jeffrey Telgarsky, and Harold Katsura.

In addition, the authors have benefited from discussions with a number of persons about events in the housing sectors covered in the Report. These persons include Robert Buckley, Steve Mayo, Piet Nankman, Ivan Tosics, Douglas Diamond, and Jozsef Hegedus. They also gained insights from the Seminar on Housing Reform in Socialist Economies held at the World Bank in June 1990.

The material and intellectual support provided by Julie Otterbein and Lee Roussel at USAID's Office of Housing and Urban Programs was instrumental to the preparation of our Report. Lastly, we gratefully acknowledge the funding for this work from The Ford Foundation and other Urban Institute sponsors.

CONTENTS

Tables

Figure

ABSTRACT

An important part of the transformation taking place in Eastern Europe from a centrally planned economic system to a competitive market paradigm involves the housing sector. In the short run reform of the housing sector eases the pain of the economic adjustment. In the long run it helps lay the foundation for a more efficient economy. This report reviews the situation as of mid-1990 in six Eastern European countries.

Although these economies grew fast in the 1970s, lagging growth in the 1980s, due to dislocations of all kinds, has spurred the impetus for market-oriented reform. These have led to some improvements in growth, but at the cost of inflation and indebtedness because of the slow pace and limited nature of the reforms.

Housing reforms have made only limited progress, although the extent of progress varies by country. Further progress depends on 1) developing a system of housing finance that makes loans available at market rates for construction and house purchasing; 2) eliminating the favored status in the housing production market still enjoyed by many of the state-operated enterprises, and 3) reforming the state rental sector by raising rents to market levels, and by introducing competitive bidding for management contracts of individual buildings.

EXECUTIVE SUMMARY

An important part of the transformation taking place in Eastern Europe from the centrally planned, "command" economic system to a competitive market paradigm involves the housing sector. This sector accounts for 4-6 percent of national income in these centrally planned economies. Their history of massive housing subsidies and arbitrarily low mortgage interest rates, combined with the lack of other consumer goods for households to spend money on, has led to substantial distortions in the housing market that have wider macroeconomic implications. And dissatisfaction with housing conditions in these countries is likely to make housing an important benchmark for judging the success of economic reform generally.

Reform of the shelter sector offers both short- and long-run benefits to the economy. In the short run, a more efficient housing sector eases the pain of the economic adjustment process by affecting both inflation and demand. In the longer run, it will help lay the foundation for a more efficient economy, spurring improvements in the financial sector, giving a larger role to private producers, and helping shape a more flexible and responsive labor market.

This report reviews the situation as of mid-1990 in six countries: Bulgaria, Czechoslovakia, Hungary, Poland, Romania, and Yugoslavia.

CPE STRUCTURE AND THE
IMPETUS FOR REFORM

In the traditional CPEs the state owned most of the productive assets of the economy and exercised control over all major economic activity through a hierarchical planning bureaucracy. Macroeconomic management was seen as the outcome of the aggregation of the microeconomic management embodied in the planning process. Most production was done by large state-owned enterprises (SOEs), whose managers were judged mainly on their ability to meet their plan quota. Bonuses and other incentives were offered to both managers and workers who met their quotas. SOEs were also mandated to make a profit, a proportion of which could be retained for enterprise use.

Prices and wages were fixed (on a cost basis) by the planners; open inflation was unknown. By establishing different sets of prices for producers and consumers, the planners could monitor enterprise performance and control demand for output. Basic goods and services were provided free or at a nominal charge.

Economic growth was strong over an extended period under this system, surpassing market economies of similar size, because of the high priority placed on investment and production. Planning also enabled these CPEs to transform their economies from an agricultural base to an industrial base in a few decades. By the 1980s high growth could not be sustained, however. Continued accumulation of capital, labor, and materials produced less and less output per unit of investment. Planning became increasingly difficult as the scale and complexity of the planning effort increased. Chronic quality problems had serious effects not only on consumers but also on enterprises. And demand and supply imbalances intensified.

A common result of attempts at market-oriented reform so far has been some improvement in growth, but at the cost of inflation and indebtedness. The slow progress has been because the limited reforms have failed to go far enough in freeing the price system and allowing increased competition. Private firms often continue to face restrictions on their scale and scope of operations, heavy taxes, and discrimination in gaining access to key inputs. State enterprises often retain privileged status in the economy, exploiting their status by appropriating income for themselves and arranging loans whether needed or not. The state of reform in the housing sector mirrors this general picture.

Hungary

For 20 years Hungary has experimented with piecemeal reforms. At each step in the process the removal of one constraint has led to recognition of another layer of constraints. As a result, although Hungary appeared to succeed in creating conditions of macroeconomic stabilization between 1968 and 1986 it did not create the basis for sustained economic growth.

Hungary's housing policies have reflected its broader economic policies. In the 1960s housing was enshrined as an entitlement, with a broad array of administrative powers exercised by the state to control housing investment as well as its allocation and pricing. In response to disappointing results, various corrective measures were introduced in 1971, 1983, and 1989 to stimulate production and reduce inefficiencies and inequalities. These partial reform measures have induced partial improvements in performance, which have succeeded in an overall movement toward market-driven operations in the housing sector.

Hungary's housing sector has performed quite well in comparison to other Eastern European countries. By 1987 the share of housing investment in total state investment outlays had reached 19 percent and housing as a share of national income has remained steady at close to 6 percent.

Today 90 percent of all new housing is for private ownership and only 10 percent for state ownership. However, the state still owns about 25 percent of all the dwelling units, including 60 percent of the stock in Budapest and 30 percent in the other towns.

Housing finance is more developed in Hungary than in the other countries because of 20 years of experimentation with indirect instruments. It includes development or construction period finance as well as take-out or mortgage financing. Reforms in 1989, in particular, moved housing finance toward market conditions, but simultaneously introduced whole new clusters of subsidies to insulate home purchasers from the impact of higher interest rates on housing affordability. Aggregate subsidies, fully accounted, amount to about 7.5 percent of national income. Reducing and rationalizing these subsidies will be central if market-oriented reform is to proceed much further.

Poland

Among CPEs Poland has a relatively long history of reform aimed at decentralizing decision-making within the economy, but it was not until 1981 that real movement away from the CPE paradigm occurred. Poor economic conditions and resistance by the administrative apparatus to the proposed scaling back of its powers, however, limited the results of the 1981 reforms. In late 1987 a second round of reform freed the economy considerably from central control, but did little to impose discipline on state-owned enterprises. The inflation and instability that followed prompted a third round of reform, the "Big Bang," which went into effect in January 1990. These new reforms are based on a convertible currency, free prices, and operational freedom for state enterprises, while severely cutting back state spending and support and imposing market rates on previously "soft" lending.

Poland has the most severe housing shortage in Eastern Europe, because of its low level of housing investment and productivity compared with other countries of similar incomes or housing deficits. In 1985 there were 18 percent more households than dwellings. The share of housing in total investment was only 13 percent in 1975. It has now risen to over 20 percent, but lagging productivity and rising costs have prevented real output from rising. About half the current housing stock is privately owned; the rest is evenly split between state-owned and cooperative housing. The 1990 reforms require public producers to borrow at commercial rates. This is causing financial difficulties for them, but should open the way for private producers to acquire labor and surplus equipment.

The majority of urban land is still owned by the state. Reform has, in principle, made these state lands available for sale and development. But direct subsidies for land development and infrastructure are still available and free or underpriced transfers of land to housing investors still take place, causing land hoarding.

In 1990 the major issue in housing finance in Poland is how to rationalize the enormous subsidy system while making housing affordable in an inflationary environment. In 1989 subsidies made up over 7 percent of government expenditures and added to inflationary pressure, even though housing costs were out of reach of many households. With respect to home ownership, the 1990 reforms raised interest rates on all new and outstanding lending, the burden of which is to be spread between the households affected and the state. Even so, many households may default on outstanding mortgages if there is a new round of inflation. In the rental sector reforms have already led to substantial rent increases, but rents still cover only one-fifth of the maintenance costs associated with state rental housing. State owners and managers of rental housing are now required to collect adequate rents to cover their costs, and further rent increases are expected as the government has indicated that rents should also cover major repairs. In July 1990, however, the next round of rent increases was postponed, so implementation of this policy is unclear.

Czechoslovakia

Market-oriented reform was not really begun in Czechoslovakia until 1985, when the major economic slump of 1981-1982 necessitated a radical revision of the economic plan and imposition of an austerity program to reduce foreign debt and cut imports. The pace of reform quickened with the political changes in 1990, but Czechoslovakia is still taking a much more cautious approach to reform than Poland or Hungary.

The housing sector in Czechoslovakia is one of the smallest in Eastern Europe, accounting for 3.4 percent of national income in 1987. Housing's share of total investment is just under 12 percent. There are acute shortages in urban areas, where the wait for housing averages about five years. Quality also is poor.

SOEs have reduced their share of housing production. They now account for 29 percent, compared with 44 percent for cooperative and 27 percent for private households, much of which is in the "second" economy or in the form of self-help. State rental housing has been available for sale since 1966, and individual ownership is permitted, up to one residence and one vacation home per individual. Owners can buy and sell homes in the private market, and land for private housing construction has been available from both local authorities and private landowners. But extensive subsidies in the housing finance market mean that house owners on average devote a very small proportion of their incomes to housing.

The rental market is similar. Apartments constructed by the state are financed entirely out of the government budget and rents have not been changed since 1964.

Discussions are now underway to develop a new housing policy that addresses some of the problems facing the sector, including additional forms of property ownership; reform of public sector housing finance (including rents, operating subsidies, and lending; and privatization of both housing and the construction industry). These reforms are likely to continue quite gradually, however, with the transition period lasting through 1995.

Yugoslavia

Among the CPEs in Eastern Europe, Yugoslavia was a pioneer in economic reform. In some respects, the country seemed to be taking the right steps. Central planning was abolished and foreigners were welcome. But in other respects the reforms did not go far enough. Spending was never fully subjected to the rigors of the market; and bureaucrats with little commercial experience made major decisions over the allocation of resources. As a result the economic growth that propelled Yugoslavia past its Eastern European counterparts in the 1960s and 1970s has come to a near standstill, prompting a more critical examination of past reforms, and more radical reforms in 1989 and 1990.

The share of housing in national income fell to 3.6 percent in 1985 and housing's share of total investment fell to 17 percent in 1985. Housing production has correspondingly fallen, until Yugoslavia now ranks near the bottom of European countries in number of dwelling units per thousand inhabitants. Housing quality varies considerably, with most housing fully equipped in some areas of the country but not in others.

Only about one-fifth of all housing was in social ownership as long ago as 1981 (the most recent census). Housing production has also been shifting away from SOEs, which produced only 32 percent of the housing in 1987, to the private sector, which now accounts for about 90 percent of non-SOE-produced housing. With reforms in 1986 and 1988, loss-making SOEs are now allowed to fail and no longer have access to easy funds for housing construction, since the government has stripped them of their welfare functions. There is little information on how private individuals produce their own housing, although some observers think that a large proportion is through self-help.

Housing in Yugoslavia is obtained primarily in one of two ways: by being granted tenancy rights for a socially owned building (with very low rents) or by purchasing or constructing a unit with private, or a mixture of private and public, funds. There is also a private rental market, but its development has been limited by strong tenant rights and massively subsidized rents in the socialized sector.

Social housing constructed for rental is financed primarily out of the income and profits of SOEs within a local district. Individuals can finance private home ownership by making a downpayment and obtaining loans through their work organizations or their banks. Mortgage and housing loans are also provided by commercial banks and savings and loan organizations. The revalorization of credit in 1987 raised the cost of servicing mortgage debt, however, putting home purchasers at a relative disadvantage compared to tenancy right holders in social housing, who pay rents far below market levels.

Raising rents is a high priority if housing reform is to progress further--not only to recover construction and maintenance costs but also as a prerequisite to any major privatization effort. Currently rents and utility prices are frozen, however, as part of the latest stabilization effort.

Bulgaria

Bulgaria's economic development has been notable in that some productive specialization has been achieved in areas where the country has some comparative advantage rather than the typical approach of simply pushing forward with heavy industry. Since the mid-1970s, however, economic progress has been slow.

Reform efforts have been slower in Bulgaria than in all the other countries covered here except Romania. Ownership of economic assets--though not of housing--remains almost entirely in the hands of the state and past reforms have been hampered by frequent reorganization of economic structures and failure to provide adequate incentives to enterprise managers. There have been some significant economic reforms, but the recent reelection of the communist party is not a vote for a radical restructuring of the Bulgarian economy.

The housing sector in Bulgaria is relatively small, accounting for 4.4 percent of national income and 12.8 percent of investment in 1985. These shares have been roughly constant through the 1980s, but production has been falling, implying falling productivity. There is a bad geographic mismatch, with vacant units in rural areas but a 10-year wait for housing in urban areas.

Ownership is 85 percent private. The remaining 15 percent is owned by municipal councils and SOEs and forms the rental stock. In 1988, 47 percent of all new housing was sponsored by SOEs, 20 percent by cooperatives, and the remaining 33 percent by the private sector. Most housing is fully equipped but with considerable deferred maintenance.

Until recently all aspects of the pricing and transfer of real estate and housing were controlled by municipal governments. This control meant that owners did not often wish to give up their current dwelling when they acquired another, and would maintain ownership of the original unit (legally or illegally) if at all possible. In April 1990 all constraints that had previously governed private housing transactions were lifted. Households can now exercise a full range of rights over housing property, including setting prices and sale terms without local government intervention. There remains little readily available information on sale prices, however, forcing households to do their own research on market prices. The National Savings Bank will still be the primary source of housing finance, but plans are to raise interest rates to market levels. Whether these measures are implemented effectively will have a lot to say about future housing reform in Bulgaria.

Romania

Romania has a history of high industrial growth, achieved by high levels of input growth rather than increasing efficiency. Strains began to appear in the economy about 1977 and, although official statistics indicate some recovery since 1983, outside observers believe the stagnation has continued. Romania has been successful at eliminating the country's foreign debt, but at the cost of outmoded technology and endemic shortages of many basic consumer goods, pushing Romania's standard or living to one of the lowest in Europe.

The economy has been one of the most rigidly controlled, and its population and new government seem among the least enthusiastic of any in Eastern Europe about moving toward a market economy.

Romania has the smallest share of resources devoted to housing of any East European country, housing production amounting to 2.3 percent of national income in 1985 and housing investment to 8.1 percent of total investment. There is a drastic housing shortage, with new units representing less than 60 percent of new households formed each year.

Housing in Romania is produced both by the socialized sector and by private individuals. The socialized sector accounted for 94 percent of all new housing in 1980, the latest year for which information is available. Housing is extremely poor in this sector, with many new apartment blocks slums even before the scaffolding is removed. Private sector construction did not formally exist before 1989. Most private construction is still carried out as small-scale part-time sidelines by workers with formal jobs in the state sector. It is confined to private land, and it faces costs that are significantly higher than construction costs in the socialized sector.

The trend in housing tenure in the 1980s has been toward increasing restrictions on private control. Restrictions on the sale of public and private dwellings were lifted in 1990, however, stimulating signs of real estate market activity.

Rents on state-owned apartments are about half as high as free-market rents. Prices for housing that is for sale are very low. Although restrictions on house purchases have been lifted, finance for such purchasing remains almost entirely in the hands of the state, with no increase in credit for the private housing sector evident.

No recent policy statement has been made on housing policy, but the following features are probable: continued strong state involvement, no significant rent increases, enlarged scope for divestiture of existing public housing and sale of new units, greater--but as yet unspecified--scope for private sector activity. But this is not a high government priority.

Transition Issues

Transition issues fall into three interrelated groups: housing finance, housing development, and the state rental sector. The greatest challenge is the need to deal with all three at the same time.

Housing Finance. The first step in developing an effective system of housing finance is to deal with the artificially cheap long-term debt that is the legacy of the past, by increasing the interest rates on existing loans. The second step is to insure that market interest rates are charged on new loans. Since affordability will be a major problem under a system in which full costs are charged for dwelling units and mortgage finance, some subsidization will probably be viewed by the state as essential. These subsidies should be explicit, however, so that the costs and relative burdens are clear. The third step is to develop a system of construction period finance, which will entail training to upgrade the underwriting skills of loan officers. The fourth step is to shift the burden of financing housing explicitly to the banking system and include all subsidies in the state budget.

Housing Development. There is general agreement that housing production by the SOEs has been inefficient. There is less recognition that currently operating private contractors are probably also inefficient. Government action is needed to eliminate impediments to private contractors by enforcing equal access to credit, building materials and labor, building sites, and competition for state-commissioned projects. Another necessity for reform is to straighten out the ownership of land parcels and to open up the flow of market information on land transactions.

State Rental Housing. Reform of the state rental sector, which ranges from 15 to 50 percent of units, is fundamental to the transformation of the housing sector. Shifting state rentals to a market basis is essential to the development of a broader rental sector. Success in this endeavor will need several steps. First, although selling units from the state inventory has been started as a way of privatizing state rental housing, care must be taken not to eliminate the rental housing market altogether. Second, the poorest families and the elderly on fixed incomes will have to be protected. Third, the housing finance system has to be able to provide financing at market rates to facilitate the purchase of units. Finally, management of the properties must be transformed to allow market competition for management contracts on individual buildings.

* * *

Officials in these countries are openly seeking advice and technical assistance from the donor community, which has already responded in Hungary and Poland and presumably will respond elsewhere also. All those working on restructuring the housing sector must remember that a minimum of several years will be required, and that each reform should be based on an appreciation of what it entails for all segments of the housing market.

Chapter One

PRESENT AT THE CREATION

The title of this introduction--coined by Dean Acheson for his book on the exciting days as U.S. Secretary of State in the early days of the cold war--captures the sense that the western world experienced during the days of the breathtaking political events in Eastern Europe that began in the fall of 1989. A new world order was being initiated after nearly a half century of stasis. These revolutionary changes foreshadow equally profound alterations to these nations' economic systems. With political liberalization is coming a fundamental shift from the centrally planned, "command" economic system to a competitive market paradigm. Each of these countries is acutely aware of the enormous challenges they confront in making both the political and economic transitions, and they are actively seeking bilateral and multilateral assistance.

This report is about the transformation of the housing sectors to a market orientation--in which households cease receiving in-kind housing benefits allocated by the state (which they received instead of higher wages) and start exercising demand for housing services through their purchasing power, and in which private individuals and firms rather than bureaucrats decide where and what type of housing units will be constructed. We review the situation as of mid-1990 in six countries: Bulgaria, Czechoslovakia, Hungary, Poland, Romania, and Yugoslavia.[1]

The housing sector--broadly defined to include both the real side (provision of serviced land, building materials and construction industries, and housing production) and the financial side (construction and mortgage financing)--deserves early and full attention in each of these countries for several reasons. Indeed, the World Bank (1989d), in the case of Poland, has identified the centrality of housing reforms to overall economic progress:

> The combination of extreme housing shortage and high subsidies . . . distorts the economy in ways that extend well beyond the boundaries of the sector. . . .

> Policy reform affecting the housing sector has the potential to benefit the economy quickly through three different circuits--the real side of the economy, the fiscal side, and the financial side. The incremental nature of housing investment makes it possible to mobilize investments quickly and in a geographically selective way....

The sector is important to the national economy--usually accounting for between 4 and 6 percent of Net Material Product (NMP).[2] Under the centrally planned systems, housing has absorbed a very large volume of subsidies, both for the development of new units and to make up the shortfall between the cost of maintenance and operation of state rental units and the meager rents paid by occupants. Mortgage lending has been conducted at arbitrarily low interest rates, which has badly distorted the primitive financial system and, when combined with the paucity of consumer goods, encouraged households to build up substantial liquidity (by preventing the state savings banks

from offering attractive rates of returns to depositors).
Perhaps most importantly, there is pervasive dissatisfaction with housing conditions in each country, most prominently evident in persistent and substantial shortfalls in the production of new units compared to the number of newly forming households.

The history of chronic housing shortages and the staggering amounts of subsidies in the centrally planned economies (CPEs) of Eastern Europe make housing a vital issue--both socially and economically--in the reform process. To households, the performance of this sector is likely to be one of the benchmarks against which the success of reform is measured. Policymakers in these countries now appear to appreciate the wider macroeconomic impacts of housing shortages and excessive subsidies. In making the transition to a market-driven housing sector, reforming governments will need economic support, cogent advice, and well-targeted technical assistance to minimize the cost of dislocations associated with reform.

The following section outlines how assisting the reform of the shelter sector offers both short- and long-term benefits to reforming CPEs. In the short run, a more efficient housing sector eases the pain of the economic adjustment process by affecting both inflation and demand. In the longer run, a well-functioning housing sector helps to lay the foundation for a more efficient economy, spurring improvements in the financial sector, giving a larger role to private producers in the housing sector, and helping shape a more flexible and responsive labor market.

The final section in this introductory chapter provides an overview of the intent and organization of the report, how its contents were compiled, and the limitations that affected the breadth and depth of our coverage of individual countries.

HOUSING AND MACROECONOMIC REFORM

A well-functioning shelter sector in a reforming CPE not only responds to long-standing social frustrations caused by persistent housing shortages. It also can play a substantial role in easing the transition to and contributing to the efficient functioning of the reformed, market-oriented economy.

As general macroeconomic restructuring proceeds, the resolution of longstanding imbalances in the economy causes many dislocations:

- Increasing inflation as newly freed prices adjust and excess liquidity, previously held in check by rationing, pushes up the money prices of scarce goods;

- Falling aggregate demand as inefficient state enterprises close or shrink their workforces to raise their competitiveness;

- Blockages caused by a financial sector that is not practiced in allocating credit by evaluating risk and return on a potential investment;

- Bottlenecks encountered as labor is unable to relocate to take up jobs in firms that achieve success in the marketplace.

The housing sector has an important contribution to make in alleviating the macroeconomic pains of reform. A well-functioning housing market can buffer the dislocations caused by economic reform in several ways:

- Households in CPEs have demonstrated strong effective demand for housing--even at very high relative prices where uncontrolled units have been available; meeting this demand can soak up liquidity to restrain inflation. It can also help maintain the level of activity in the economy during the slowdown associated with restructuring;

- Reduction of subsidies for housing can decrease government expenditure and lessen inflationary pressure through smaller budget deficits--while increasing efficiency within the economy by making households face the true cost of housing;

- A strong housing market can provide impetus for a more efficient and innovative financial sector;

- Where the housing market has been freed from state control, private construction firms have responded by increasing their share of housing production;

- A more efficient housing market can improve labor mobility and ease the redistribution of labor within the economy that will flow out of restructuring.

These are the *potential* pay-offs of careful adjustment and reform in the housing sector. We discuss each in turn.

We do not mean to imply that simply moving to a free-market system in the sector will produce nothing but positive results. Indeed, there is the danger that pursuing a "big bang" solution could impose tremendous costs on those segments of society--people on fixed incomes or reliant on the state for support--which are least able to cope with large price rises. In looking at the potential benefits of a well-functioning housing market, we also attempt to underline the dangers which must be avoided along the way.

Restraining Inflationary Pressure

A key objective of governments in reforming CPEs is to keep inflation under control; prices will tend to rise (pushed up by households' forced savings previously held in check by rationing) as they are released from administrative control.[3] Indeed, a primary result of the decontrol on prices in Poland in 1990 was an initial severe rise in the price of serviced land, building materials, and credit, which has drastically cut effective demand for housing. The rise in the prices of these goods is exacerbated by their inelastic supply. When price constraints are removed, the newly freed prices of goods such as serviced land and housing "overshoot" their long-run equilibrium price until the supply side of the market catches up with demand. Thus, developing a supply side response--equalizing access to credit, materials, and labor for private construction firms compared to state owned enterprises (SOEs); increasing the supply of serviced land for development--is an important step toward achieving a well-functioning housing sector.

Although some supply responses are necessarily long term (such as restructuring the construction industry), some actions can ease supply in the short term. For example, most CPEs have large numbers of housing units under construction by private households, which could be completed if restrictions against owning multiple properties were lifted and if regulations governing private sales were eased. This could boost the supply of housing available and under-cut some of the overshooting associated with freeing previously controlled prices.

If these problems of overshooting prices and poor supply response can be dampened, a reformed shelter sector can contribute to inflationary restraint by soaking up some of the liquid monetary holdings of households. The housing market offers households a commodity that is in high demand both as a consumption good and as an investment asset; the "free" market for housing (with prices, in Poland, 2 to 3 times the cost of construction) shows it is a commodity for which they are willing to pay full costs or more (World Bank 1990). This demand for housing can soak up savings held (often outside the financial system) by households that have long been kept from fulfilling their preferences by the unavailability or low quality of consumption goods. In the early stages of reform, before the structural changes needed to satisfy consumer demand have taken place, keeping liquidity in the economy down improves the ability of the government to restrain inflation. This reduces the need to curb inflation through macroeconomic means, such as forcing down real wages, raising interest rates, or cutting demand through higher prices.

Reduction of Subsidies

Access to housing and its financing in traditional CPEs have always been administratively controlled (except for a small part of the sector where households operate outside the state system). Structural impediments inherent in the planners' policy choices (i.e., treating housing as a "non-productive" good and keeping the cost of housing to households artificially low) and the incentive systems employed in CPEs (which emphasized production targets rather than responding to demands from the market) acted as a brake on any improvement in sector performance. As a result, extensive systems of subsidies have been established to keep official housing costs low as a counterbalance to the persistent problem of inadequate housing supply.

Creation of a well-functioning housing market offers governments the opportunity to cut subsidies (thereby restraining some of the excess demand caused by artificially low prices and the inflationary pressure which subsidies may bring)--with the bonus of improved efficiency in the housing market. Housing subsidies, such as rents and utility charges that do not reflect the full cost of housing and services, up-front capital subsidies, and below-market interest rates, contribute to inflationary pressure when they are not well-designed or targeted to low-income households. Such subsidies not only add significantly to the government budget deficit, but also generate excess cash balances for households who receive the subsidies and do not face the full cost of housing.

Subsidies supporting the operation of state-owned rental housing, which are not strongly linked to household incomes and needs, form a significant part of government budgets. In Poland, raising rents in state housing to cover upkeep and utility costs would reduce central government spending; in 1989, these subsidies accounted for almost 4 percent of government expenditure (World Bank 1990).

Other subsidies for housing also form a large portion of government expenditure. In Hungary, Buckley et al. (1990) estimate that subsidies for housing equals 7 percent of GDP. One-third of these were to cover the cost of below-market loans for housing issued by state banks.

Rationalization of these subsidies would raise the proportion of household income spent on housing from current low levels (less than 5 percent for most households in state-supplied housing) to levels close to the 15 percent spent by households in other countries with similar levels of development. Eliminating housing subsidies--or at least designing them better--not only results in lower budget deficits which would ease inflationary pressure, but also brings about a more market-based allocation of housing. Given the size of the housing sector, both these effects are important contributions to successful implementation of the reform process.

However, the difficulties and resistance past and present changes to the system of housing subsidies have encountered indicates that restructuring subsidies will not be simple. Attempts to raise rents in both Poland and Hungary without reforming other aspects of the social welfare system have been defeated or greatly scaled back. It seems clear that constructing some sort of "safety net" to protect those most vulnerable to the effects of higher rents will be an important step to take before market-oriented rents can be considered.

A similar problem exists with the reform of subsidies for housing purchase. There are important equity issues to be faced over the benefits granted to households who secured low-cost mortgages in the past and those who will now face market interest rates. In Poland, for example, all existing mortgages were converted to floating rate terms as part of the reform of the financial system. Where state lenders cannot raise the interest rates on existing mortgages with very low, fixed interest rates (as in Hungary), alternative solutions, such as taxing the benefits conferred by the subsidy, can be used to even out benefits.

Maintaining Aggregate Demand

Another benefit of a well-functioning housing market is the sector's stable demand--even as restructuring in other sectors depresses overall demand. Thus, an efficient housing market offers reforming economies a sector with strong demand and high domestic content--one that can help maintain an adequate level of economic activity while other sectors undergo recession as part of their adaptation to a more competitive economic environment.

In Poland, the freeing of prices under the reform program led to an initial burst of inflation as prices sought their correct levels. These higher prices translated into lower output and rising unemployment. However, demand for housing, once the overshooting of high interest rates and building materials prices have begun to decline, should return to its former high levels. Over 400,000 units of housing sit uncompleted because of lack of financing and materials or because of regulatory delays (World Bank 1990). With cost-effective, moderate interventions, such as relaxation of regulatory restrictions or clearing of key production bottlenecks (lack of infrastructure, shortages of a few key materials), the completion of these units could be accelerated. A careful inventory of uncompleted units would be required to identify those with the greatest pay-off. The resulting production would help stabilize the construction industry, which is in a severe downturn and requires large-scale restructuring.

Housing demand in Hungary has also declined as households face high purchase prices (relative to reported incomes) for housing and 25 percent mortgage interest rates. However, the World Bank (1989c) reports substantial potential demand for housing, which the current producers (SOEs and small-scale builders) are unable to produce in sufficient quantity. One sign of the potential demand is the sustained high level of production of self-built housing units. Also, although Hungarian housing demand based on official statistics appears weak, little account is taken of income which households receive from "second economy" sources. There appears to be much activity that could be spurred by a better matching of supply (in terms of housing type and quality) with household demand.

Thus, in the two countries that have taken up the reform effort most fully, the shelter sector appears poised to act as a source of economic activity during periods of economic retrenchment. In the Polish case, where the "shock" approach to reform has the potential of sending production in the economy into a steep decline, the countercyclical benefits of unmet demand for housing can play a role in lessening the negative impact of reform.

Improved Financial Intermediation

With a well-functioning housing market, the financial system will be both broadened and deepened (soaking up excess liquidity in the process) as households face stronger incentives to save in financial form and finance the purchase of housing.

Households will be less likely to save in financial form if their assets do not retain their value over time (e.g., if the real interest rate on deposits is negative) or if the future availability of goods for purchase with savings is doubtful (in which case they will consume what is available today because it may be in short supply tomorrow). The achievement of positive real incentives for saving is not a sufficient condition for mobilizing financial savings--adequate supply response from the productive side of the economy must also take place.

In a period of economic change as is being experienced in Eastern Europe, housing-linked contract savings schemes offer a potential means of increasing the proportion of savings held in financial form. Such schemes not only help borrowers overcome imperfections in the capital market (which are likely to exist in reforming CPEs), but also can increase households' motivation for saving in financial form if participation in the scheme establishes priority in the housing queue. This would obviously be an attractive feature to households whose previous savings efforts made little impact on their access to housing. Struyk and Friedman (1989) found exactly these positive relationships in an analysis of a contract savings scheme in India.

There are certainly efficiency gains associated with channeling an increased proportion of national savings through the financial system (though quantitative gains are less certain--see below). Greater intermediation by the financial system allows more productive investment by more efficiently matching capital with borrowers--if the credit allocation mechanisms of the financial system are able to accurately assess risk and return of different borrowers.

The measured savings rate (based mainly on savings in financial form) is likely to be low while real interest rates on deposits are negative and while the accumulation of savings does not improve access to desired consumer goods or housing. In Poland, where such conditions persisted during the early 1980s, the savings rate declined from 17 percent of GDP in 1981 to 8 percent in 1984 (World Bank 1987). With the return of positive real rates of interest on deposits and allocation of housing and other goods through a market-oriented price mechanism, households again have reason to accumulate cash balances within the financial system; the early evidence from the 1990 reforms is that households are responding positively.

Use of market-determined interest rates also places greater demands on the financial sector that will require improved techniques of risk assessment and lending instrument design. Lenders in CPEs, particularly mortgage lenders, have not been required to make decisions about credit allocation between competing borrowers and have borne little risk of default by the borrowers because of the state's willingness to grant subsidies to assure repayment. Changes in Eastern Europe which move the financial system toward a more businesslike and competitive distribution of credit (both for housing and other purposes) will improve the efficiency of investment--but will also introduce the risk of default.

Demand for housing finance would also provide incentives for other financial institutions to get involved in the sector, providing competition to the existing source of mortgage finance (usually a state bank which previously held a monopoly over the mortgage business). Eastern European governments, led by Poland and Hungary, are removing the monopoly privileges for housing finance granted to state savings banks. However, without an active housing market, there will be little incentive for other financial institutions to attempt to compete in the mortgage lending business.

Expanded Private Sector Activity

Improved functioning of the housing sector serves as a strong incentive for private enterprise to play a larger role in housing supply, with likely gains in productivity and efficiency. The shelter sector is also marked by strong forward and backward linkages in the economy. Thus, increased private sector activity in housing can act as a spur to private sector activity elsewhere in the economy.

In most Eastern European countries, neither state nor private producers are operating at an efficient scale: state producers are large, heavily subsidized conglomerates that can only develop housing projects with hundreds of units on very large sites. Private producers are small, under-capitalized, and build mainly single-family units for individual households with adequate resources to self-finance the unit. With the implementation of reforms described above--increased incentives for saving, improved allocation of credit, affordable lending instruments--to convert latent demand for housing into effective demand, private activity in the shelter sector should grow to meet this demand.

Indeed, this has been the case in Hungary, where the ability of households to purchase housing provided by private construction firms at free-market prices and the elimination of preferential take-out financing for state housing has led to an increase in private sector share of housing construction from 62 percent in 1975 to 89 percent in 1986 (Matras 1989a).

Improved Labor Mobility

In market economies, labor seeks its highest return by moving to jobs with higher wages offered by more productive firms and industries. Market clearing in this case assumes households having to change locations can obtain housing at a price that still allows their real incomes to rise. If housing is too costly to allow this movement, two kinds of responses can be expected: (1) wages offered will rise further to compensate for the cost of housing; or (2) more housing will be supplied, lowering the cost of housing. Mayo and Stein (1988) report that, in most market economies, housing shortages are eliminated relatively quickly through increased supply.

In CPEs, movement of labor has historically been low. Households face difficulty in finding new housing if they move and are less willing to give up housing they already occupy. Instead, households bear higher housing costs than they would optimally choose, as manifested by relatively high housing prices for those units which do change hands, long commutes to work, and poor housing conditions (evidenced by poor quality construction, lack of amenities, and overcrowding). Consequently, there is upward pressure on money wages to compensate for these higher housing costs; wages may often exceed their competitive level.

Mayo and Stein (1988) find that disequilibrium in the housing market in Poland (as evidenced by housing prices that greatly exceed costs and levels of investment in housing below that found in similar countries) depresses labor mobility. Econometric analysis indicates the influence of housing shortages is large, with most firms responding with higher wages to make up for the costs of the housing shortage. Similar anecdotal evidence from other countries suggests that housing shortages were often the key determinant in households' decisions to move; state enterprises in Hungary were often able to attract workers, not simply by offering higher wages, but by offering access to housing.

One of the key components of economic reform is a reshaping of the distribution of labor and a more flexible labor market. In Hungary, for example, at least 200,000 workers are expected to change jobs, half of them moving to a different industry (The Economist 1988). Housing shortages in CPEs are a major impediment to such adjustments, especially if the new job is in another city. Mayo and Stein's findings provide strong evidence for Poland that major distortions in the labor market are caused by housing shortages in growing areas. In short, efficient restructuring of the labor force in response to economic reform will not take place unless housing is available to accommodate those workers who wish to move to areas of labor shortage.

REPORT OVERVIEW AND ORGANIZATION

This report provides a starting point for those who want to be informed about housing conditions in Eastern European countries and about the initial steps they are taking in the transition to market-oriented systems. We compiled the information presented from existing papers and reports, from interviews with knowledgeable staff at the World Bank and the International Monetary Fund and from discussions with experts from Eastern Europe, some of whom we met at conferences and others who visited The Urban Institute's offices in Washington. One of us spent a month on a World Bank-USAID housing mission to Hungary to gather first-hand information.

We found sharp differences in the materials available which mirror the different lengths of time they have been experimenting with economic reforms and different degrees of participation in international organizations such as the World Bank, IMF, and United Nations Economic Commission for Europe (ECE). Much more analysis and data are available for the housing sector in Hungary and Poland (which have been recently visited by housing-related missions of the World Bank) than for the other countries. In these cases, we relied on official statistics and available published and unpublished descriptive materials which, though not as complete as the World Bank studies, do provide a good basis for understanding the housing sector in each country. Data on Bulgaria and Czechoslovakia were acquired through UN and national sources, with additional information obtained from a recent World Bank conference and published English-language journal articles. Romania, though a nominal member of the World Bank and IMF, has not actively participated for several years. In addition, much of the official data reported during the Ceausescu regime is now deemed to be unreliable. However, we were able to obtain several recent unpublished papers which provide valuable insight into the Romanian housing sector. Finally, in the case of Yugoslavia, we relied mainly on UN and national sources, as little work has been done by the World Bank in the housing sector in recent years nor have English-language journals carried many articles.

This report has three main parts. Part I gives background material. Chapter 1 inventories the reasons why housing reform is so important for Eastern European countries. Chapter 2 sketches the broad structure of the macroeconomic changes underway. This is the context in which housing reforms are or will be occurring. To orient the reader to the six countries covered in the report, chapter 3 presents comparative information on their economies and housing sectors.

Part II has six chapters, one for each country, beginning with Hungary and Poland--the two about which we have the most information. Each of these chapters can be read alone, and each begins with a quick review of the economic situation and reforms underway and then turns to a review of housing sector developments. This review emphasizes how far advanced the reforms are particularly in Hungary and to a lesser degree in Poland compared with the other nations, and makes clear how everyone interested in the transformation of the housing sector can learn from their experiences.

Part III discusses a set of "transition problems" that each of these countries will face in some form. For clarity these problems are grouped into three major categories--housing finance, housing development, and the state rental sector-- although in reality the categories are interrelated. The problems confronted are daunting; but, if thoughtfully and systematically addressed, they appear within the competence of these nations to resolve.

Notes, chapter one

1. With the reunification of East and West Germany under way as this report was being prepared, the reform of the East German economy is following a path not available to other East European countries. Because of its special circumstances, East Germany has not been included among the countries examined in this report.

2. NMP is a national income measure similar to the Gross Domestic Product (GDP) measure used in market economies, but only accounts for the material value of output--i.e., NMP is equal to GDP less excess value of nonmaterial services (domestic and net imported); consumption of fixed capital; and transfer costs of existing fixed capital (see United Nations, 1986). Thus, banking, health, education, public administration, and defense are excluded. The IMF (1989a) estimates that MNP in Hungary in 1988 was equal to 82 percent of GDP and in Poland in 1987 to 83 percent of GDP.

In the case of the contribution of housing to NMP, national accounts based on NMP refer only to housing investment and do not include any value for the flow of housing services households derive from their dwelling.

3. However this effect will be dampened to the extent households believe their savings held in currency act as an effective store of value. This consideration explains the move to make the zloty convertible in Poland in January 1990 and the lack of an inflationary spending burst following the conversion of Ostmarks in East Germany to convertible Deutschemarks in July 1990.

Chapter Two

CENTRALLY PLANNED ECONOMIES AND REFORM

Over the past 20 years, the centrally planned economies (CPEs) of Eastern Europe have been struggling to find ways to improve their systems of resource allocation. Although these CPEs differ in size, level of economic development, and how the central planning system is implemented, their reforms share many common characteristics and experiences. The early reforms improved some aspects of economic performance. They also exposed latent problems in the economy (such as repressed inflation or external imbalances), which created pressures for retrenchment (particularly in the early stages of the reform process) or increasingly radical reform (as seen through the 1980s and culminating in the massive changes of 1989).

This chapter summarizes the evolution of the CPEs and the general path of reform.

EVOLUTION OF THE PLANNED ECONOMY

Following World War II, the countries in Eastern Europe adopted an economic system modeled after the central planning system developed in the USSR during the 1920s and 1930s. These systems differed significantly from market-driven economies in their mechanisms for making economic choices.

Characteristics of Traditional CPEs

In the traditional CPE, the state owned most of the productive assets of the economy. State ownership was virtually complete in the industrial and natural resource sectors. Only the sectors characterized by small-scale operations-- such as agriculture, retailing, personal services, and housing--had significant private ownership.

The state exercised control over all major economic activity through a hierarchical planning bureaucracy. Other instruments of economic control, such as prices and fiscal policy, were of only secondary importance. Macroeconomic management was seen as the outcome of the aggregation of the microeconomic management embodied in the planning process. Medium-term plans (usually covering five years) set out the general directions of development within the economy. Annual plans specified how the objectives of the medium-term plans were to be achieved.

The national planning agency, in consultation with the policymakers of the country, developed broad plans that set national priorities for the year. These plans were then developed in greater detail by regional planning agencies and functional ministries (usually organized by industry). These lower level bodies specified production orders for individual state-owned enterprises (SOEs) under their control.[1] At all stages in the planning process, the parties negotiated in order to devise a plan which set out realistic targets. A similar process occurred to specify the levels of inputs the production managers would be allocated to meet their production targets. Managers were judged mainly on their ability to meet their plan quota. Bonuses and other incentives were offered to both managers and workers for meeting their target. Enterprises were also mandated to operate at a profit. Usually, a proportion of profits in excess of a specified norm could be retained by the enterprise for its own use.

The state also exercised control over international trade; dealings with foreign purchasers and suppliers were carried out by state-owned foreign trade organizations (FTOs). The volume and distribution of trade was specified by the planning agency to match the levels of domestic production set out in the remainder of the plan. Like other state enterprises, FTOs were evaluated based on fulfillment of plan requirements.

The CPE was used by the state to achieve a set of key policy objectives: full employment, stable prices, and rapid industrialization and economic growth. Plan targets were set to create a steady demand for labor and provide job security. What unemployment did exist was attributable mainly to temporary dislocations resulting from the orderly transfer of labor that was part of the planned development of the economy.

Prices and wages were fixed (on a cost basis) by the planners, with occasional revisions to compensate for large changes in economic structure or strategy; open inflation did not exist. By establishing different sets of prices for producers and consumers, the planners to were able to monitor enterprise performance and control demand for output. Basic goods and services, such as food, education, medical care, and housing, were provided free of charge or at very low cost.

Economic growth in CPEs over the long term has been strong, surpassing that of market economies of similar size. In addition, control of the economy through central planning allowed the CPEs to transform their economies from an agricultural to an industrial base in the space of a few decades.

Operational Problems of CPEs

Despite their impressive achievements, several features of the structure and operation of traditional CPEs generated a set of internal conflicts:

- Information asymmetries between planners and state producers;

- Price system rigidities;

- State policies that hindered labor market flexibility;

- Credit market access that did not reflect the true cost of capital;

- Insulation from foreign trade influences;

- Lack of consumer input into planning priorities.

The economic system was poorly equipped to resolve these conflicts, which reflected divergences between the intentions of the planners and the incentives--both intended/explicit and unintended/implicit--created by the economic system.[2] These divergences made it progressively more difficult to maintain high levels of economic performance.

Each of these features is discussed briefly below.

INFORMATION ASYMMETRIES

The formulation of economywide plans placed impossible information requirements on the planning agencies. As a result, plans were often drawn up based on data about production levels, plant capacity, and input requirements as reported by enterprise managers (and their supporting agencies). This information was distorted because the managers, evaluated on their ability to fulfill plan targets, had powerful incentives to overstate their input requirements and understate their ability to meet the targets, in order to reduce the effort required and to hedge against potential production bottlenecks.

PRICE SYSTEM

Information flows related to the planning process occurred within the state bureaucracy; the use of prices to convey information about the supply and demand of a commodity was almost nonexistent. Planners had two reasons for trying to keep prices unchanged. First, carrying out a general revision of prices for thousands of goods required a massive analytic effort. Second, since inflation had been a problem under previous economic systems, price stability was important as a symbol of a CPE's success. Prices on key commodities were usually controlled by the central planners. But this control was by no means universal. Enterprises were often able to introduce "new" products that were not in fact new but carried higher prices. This process, which went on with little review by the planning authorities, enabled enterprises to capture additional financial resources to pay for bonuses and other non-wage incentives. Thus, prices did not reflect consumption preferences and production possibilities, but rather bureaucratic maneuvering by enterprises and the planning agency.

LABOR MARKET

State objectives of full employment and job security were met by holding down wage differentials (which did not, therefore, accurately reflect labor productivity differences) and drastically limiting the restructuring of the labor force of a CPE. In fact, the desire to protect jobs was so strong that most CPEs had no mechanisms for closing loss-making or bankrupt enterprises; enterprises continued to operate with subsidies or were absorbed into larger, more profitable enterprises. In addition, without the power to use flexible wages or the threat of dismissal as incentives, enterprises were forced to rely on bonuses and other compensation (such as housing) to reward workers. At the same time, the system incentives encouraged enterprises to hoard excess workers as a hedge against failing to meet the plan target. This created apparent labor "shortages" in the economy even though there was under-employment of workers within most enterprises. These labor allocation problems were aggravated by labor immobility of workers caused by housing shortages due to lack of investment in the housing sector and rent control.

CREDIT CONTROL

The pricing and allocation of capital was also divorced from considerations of supply and demand. Investment decisions were based mainly on requirements for meeting the plan targets as reported by the enterprises. Wage earners with savings were forced to hold them either as cash or in deposit accounts that paid negligible interest. Enterprise demand for investment capital was met by grants from the state (from profits that the enterprises had to return almost totally to the state and by taxes on consumption) or by low-cost or interest-free loans from state banks using artificially cheap funds from their depositors or onlending from the central bank. Not surprisingly, enterprise managers showed a marked preference for creating excess capacity and building new facilities rather than upgrading existing plant and equipment.

FOREIGN TRADE

FTOs often had monopoly control over the trade of key commodities and were, like other state enterprises, preoccupied with achieving their plan target. The other state enterprises, which relied on the FTOs for supplying inputs or marketing their output, had little influence over FTO operations. "Price equalization," using a variety of taxes and subsidies, was used to offset the difference between the prevailing world price and the plan-mandated domestic price. Domestic producers were thus isolated from changes in world markets. They did not respond to changing world prices of raw material inputs and operated independently of changes in the prices or quality of the products of their overseas competitors.

SUPPLY-DRIVEN PRODUCTION

Consumers played a negligible role in the planning process. Changes in consumer preferences or mismatches between supply and demand, which in any case had to be passed through a long chain from retailers to planners, were often ignored. The enterprises, ministries, and planners faced powerful incentives to maintain the status quo and state plans gave more weight to investment than to consumption and to heavy industry than to consumer goods and housing. These operational problems led to strains.

One source of strain was the difference between the planners' choice of development strategy and the apparent preferences of consumers. The development strategy of the CPEs relied mainly on mobilizing increasing amounts of capital, labor, and material rather than efficient use of the factors already in production. Growth was achieved by expanding heavy industry and restricting output growth of consumer goods, social services, and housing. Other key sectors (such as agriculture) also lagged because of unfavorable relative prices set by the planners and the consequent lack of producer incentives.

A second source of strain was the inherent difficulty of putting together the national plan. The sheer scope of the planning process and its imperfect information base made failures in meeting the specified production targets inevitable. "Correcting" targets for enterprises without altering aggregate targets for particular industries or sectors led to mismatches in supply and demand that were magnified as their effects rippled throughout the economy. Without price flexibility to absorb this pressure, the adjustment had to be carried out through rationing of certain goods, limitations on investment or availability of subsidies, and tighter controls on wage bills.

CPEs offered individuals the security of assured employment, an egalitarian wage structure, and stable prices. But this security led to an inflexible labor market that increased the difficulties of altering the mix of output in the economy--a problem compounded by the lack of a price system to respond to demand and supply differences. Consumers were seldom able to use their wages for consumption--particularly for consumer goods and low-priced (but extremely scarce) housing; forced savings and underconsumption were the result. Both enterprises and consumers were forced to look outside the formal CPE structure to satisfy their preferences (albeit in risky and inefficient ways). Enterprises resorted to building up reserves of inputs that were not necessary for their immediate production needs; producing their own equipment and inputs on an inefficient, small scale; or obtaining materials through informal trade with other enterprises or on the black market. These and other actions (such as building new plants rather than modernizing existing factories) all caused the actual operation of the economy to deviate from the path the planners had marked. Consumers resorted to boycotting low-quality goods produced under the plan, queueing for goods not produced in sufficient quantity, or paying a premium to black market suppliers who provided goods in short supply in the formal economy.

Impetus for Change

The high priority placed on investment and production in the central plans allowed CPEs initially to grow rapidly. However, the high growth rates of the 1970s could not be maintained through the 1980s (see table 2.1), as continued accumulation of capital, labor, and materials produced less and less output per unit of investment. The limits of the growth that could be attained by pouring in additional inputs without control over the productivity of their use were being reached. Further, effective management of these additional resources became increasingly difficult as

Table 2.1　ECONOMIC GROWTH IN EASTERN EUROPEAN CPEs--NET MATERIAL PRODUCT (average annual real percentage change)

	1970-80	1980-88
Bulgaria	7.1	4.4
Czechoslovakia	5.1	3.0
Hungary[a]	5.4	2.3
Poland	8.9	2.0
Romania	8.6	4.7
Yugoslavia[a]	5.8	0.6

Source: EIU (various), World Bank (1982).

a. Growth rates for GDP.

the scale and complexity of the planning effort required to control the economy increased.

In addition, the inability of CPEs to solve chronic quality problems in the production of goods and services--which translate into unsold goods remaining on the shelf and inability to export production to foreign markets--had serious effects on both consumers and enterprises. Households were unable to use their increasing cash holdings to purchase higher quality consumer goods. Enterprises encountered reduced labor productivity because of the need for frequent maintenance and repair.

Finally, supply and demand imbalances became increasingly persistent--sometimes lasting for years. Again, this affected both households and enterprises. Households could not spend as much of their income as they desired; enterprises had production runs interrupted and faced long time lags in completing investment projects. These mismatches were rooted not only in the structure of the CPE itself, but in the priorities set by the planners; shortages of housing, transportation, and social infrastructure resulted from conscious decisions to restrain investment in those sectors. The IMF (1989a) summarized the difficulties in terms of five structural problems:

- Increasingly distorted prices and the bureaucratic allocation of resources led to a pattern of production and trade which did not reflect the economy's comparative advantage.

- Households and enterprises were constantly in a state of microeconomic disequilibrium as revealed by queueing for goods, trading in the black market, and oversupply of unsalable products. The production preferences of enterprises and planners dominated the functioning of the CPE to the exclusion of the demand preferences of the consuming households.

- The nature of the planning process and inadequate incentives for efficiency led to hoarding and wasteful use of raw material and other inputs.

- A rigid labor market and bureaucratic allocation of capital helped keep the basic structure of the economy frozen, significantly reducing the scope for and speed of resource reallocation.

- Isolation from the world market and lack of efficiency incentives, combined with the inefficiencies of bureaucratically directed resource allocation, led to a slow rate of technological progress and slowed the growth of combined factor productivity.

The realization that central planning was becoming increasingly unable to deliver continued high rates of growth was the main motivation for reform in the CPEs. However, these reform efforts, some of which date from the 1950s, did not immediately focus on the market system as the solution.

THE REFORM PROCESS

The process of reform in CPEs has occurred in two main stages: initial attempts to "perfect" the planning process, followed by movement towards introducing market forces into the economy to take over the allocative tasks of the planners. This section examines each of the two approaches and concludes with an overview of where the reform process has led to date.

Perfecting the Planning System

The first steps in overhauling the economic management system usually involved attempts to decentralize decision-making, allowing enterprises to play a stronger role and scaling back the role of the central planners. The number of performance targets was reduced and the absolute control of the planners over production was loosened. The premise behind this type of reform was that under the old system the enterprises did not have enough autonomy to operate efficiently. Since increased autonomy did not address the basic causes of imbalance in the economy, however, enterprises still did not face adequate incentives and the reforms failed to produce many positive results.

The natural reaction to this failure was to reform the planning apparatus. Control by the planners was reestablished as a dominant feature of the economy, backed by a variety of changes: a streamlined planning bureaucracy; more clearly defined assignments of tasks to participants in the system; more detailed economic analysis to set prices and decide on allocations; greater use of taxes and bonuses to fine-tune the incentive system. These attempts to exercise even tighter and more "rational" control over the economy, which also failed to produce positive results, were often implemented in a cyclical fashion, as proponents of each method built on the failings of the other. Hungary, for example, experienced two reform cycles between 1954 and 1964. A similar pattern occurred in Poland, where a large decentralization effort was put into effect in 1956, followed by major "improvements" to the planning system in 1973. The failure of these types of reforms led economic policy makers to see that the problems were systemic, and that effective reform would have to reintroduce market mechanisms so that prices reflected real relative scarcities.

Market-Oriented Reform

Market-oriented reform has proceeded at different paces and in different forms in Eastern Europe. Hungary and Poland have moved the farthest through the reform process and best illustrate the breadth of approaches and experience and the difficulties that arise in trying to sustain market-oriented reform.[3]

A common result of these early attempts at market-oriented reform has been some improvement in growth, but at the cost of increasing inflation and indebtedness as limited reforms failed to go far enough in freeing the price system and allowing increased competition. Private firms often continued to face restrictions on their scale and scope of operation, heavy taxes, and discrimination in gaining access to key inputs. State enterprises often retained privileged status in the economy. Their monopolistic status meant that no enterprise could realistically be shut down. Knowing that the government would always bail them out, the enterprises faced a "soft budget constraint" and acted accordingly. Many enterprises appropriated their income for themselves--higher wages for workers and bigger bonuses for managers--and arranged loans whether needed or not. Clearly, doing away with central planning and turning state enterprises loose is not enough to bring about true market reform in CPEs.

The IMF (1989a) has identified certain basic requirements for successful market-oriented reform:

- Economic agents must be free to respond to market signals, including allowing private firms to operate on an equal footing with state enterprises, opening state monopolies to competition, and allowing inefficient enterprises to fail;

- Appropriate markets must be created so that prices find market-clearing levels;

- Instruments of macroeconomic control--monetary and fiscal policy--must be developed to replace the planning apparatus as it is dismantled.

Translating these requirements into reality requires extensive changes in the institutional and economic relationships in the CPE. We review the major ones briefly.

REFORMING STATE ENTERPRISES

Along with the increased authority and improved incentives that reform brings to state enterprises, greater financial discipline must also be imposed. The bureaucratic structure of the planning system and residual price controls need to be removed to ensure that authority--and responsibility--for decision-making devolves to the enterprises. The issue of ownership is perhaps key to enforcing financial discipline and getting market incentives to work. The state has been unable to effectively represent society's interest in the efficient use of resources by its enterprises. Turning enterprises over to their workers runs the risk of the enterprise choosing short-run wage increases (and eventual decapitalization) over long-run profit maximization. Privatization, through the auction of shares and establishment of joint ventures, seems to offer the best opportunity for solving incentive issues and enforcing efficient performance on state enterprises, although the lack of functioning capital markets and shortage of domestic capital will limit the pace at which these privatizations can be conducted. Poland has passed a law authorizing the conversion of public-sector enterprises into other forms of ownership. Hungary has established a National Property Agency to run its privatization program.[4]

During the transition other steps can be taken to increase market pressures on state enterprises. Restrictions on entry into the market by new domestic enterprises (particularly cooperatives and private firms), existing enterprises, and foreign suppliers can be lifted. Large monopolistic enterprises can be broken up into smaller units (where scale considerations do not make this is economically infeasible). Subsidies, cheap credit, government guarantees on bank borrowing, and tax concessions, can be eliminated so that loss-making enterprises are no longer kept alive through public support.

REVIVING THE PRIVATE SECTOR

The restrictions previously placed on private enterprises--which not only taxed them punitively and limited the size and scope of their operations, but also placed then at a disadvantage in gaining access to capital, foreign exchange, raw materials, and labor--need to be significantly relaxed or removed altogether. Just as effective reform in the state sector requires the government to give up its control over the operation of state industries, so must the government give up its hold over private firms. Being able to compete with the state sector does not mean much if private firms have less freedom to make decisions than their state-owned counterparts.

Particular changes which CPEs can undertake to allow the private sector to develop include: creating company laws that allow establishment of new enterprises without the need for licenses or other restrictions on their operations; giving equal treatment under the tax laws for state and private enterprises; loosening significantly or lifting licensing restrictions on international trade and domestic investment. For example, Hungary and Poland have loosened restrictions on the size of private firms (in terms of employees); Yugoslavia and Czechoslovakia still maintain tight restrictions on their size (The Economist 1989b).

PRICE REFORM

Neither real competition between state and private enterprises nor profit-based incentive systems that reflect the underlying resource scarcities in the economy will be possible until prices are set by market forces.

The optimal pace of price reform, however, remains an open question. Price revisions were often part of early, limited reform efforts but produced few results. First, planners lacked sufficient information to "get the prices right." Second, without changing the incentive system or introducing competition and financial discipline, the state enterprises that were adversely affected by the price changes were usually able to negotiate subsidies and tax exemptions which vitiated the effects of reform. For these reasons, more comprehensive price liberalization--such as that currently being undertaken in Poland--may be the best approach. However, this more drastic approach also carries dangers. Wholesale freeing of prices in CPEs characterized by significant supply constraints may set off an inflationary wage-price spiral. In addition, rapid price restructuring combined with the imposition of financial discipline on state enterprises may result in widespread insolvency throughout the state sector. Although some countries (particularly in Latin America) have learned to live with conditions of high inflation and economic instability, these adverse side-effects present an acute danger in CPEs (long accustomed to economic stability) which could derail the reform process.

Most CPEs have moved forward cautiously by relaxing controls on many goods, while reserving fixed prices for "key" goods provided by the state (usually prices on staple food and housing). The danger with these implicit subsidies is that they tend to become fixed in the expectations of urban households and perpetuate significant distortions in the economy.

The current round of reform in Poland and Hungary is taking price liberalization more seriously than previous attempts. However, the rest of Eastern Europe is proceeding much more cautiously with their price liberalization efforts.

WAGE REFORM AND THE LABOR MARKET

Reform of the labor market entails giving state enterprises greater control over their workforce and its wages while guarding against wage inflationary growth in excess of productivity gains. Most CPEs have attempted to do this through imposition of confiscatory taxes on wage bill increases over set levels. However, this approach has failed in two respects: poorly performing enterprises have been able to negotiate relief from these penalties while other enterprises have been unable to reward their workforce for gains in productivity in excess of the set limits.

Measures to improve mobility in the labor market have been hampered by the lack of information on labor demand and the chronic shortage of housing (in part due to the continued massive subsidization of state housing). State enterprises that desire to restructure their workforces have also encountered stiff resistance from the public and from trade unions. In combination with the delinking of wages and productivity, a situation of excess demand for skilled labor, underemployment in the rest of the workforce, and limited geographic labor mobility has been perpetuated. Measures to loosen these constraints, such as establishing national unemployment insurance schemes and increasing the supply of housing in labor-constrained areas, are required to develop a more efficient labor market.

MACROECONOMIC CONTROL

Loosening microeconomic control over the components of the economy means governments in CPEs will have lost their traditional tools of macroeconomic control. Along with the other changes that reform brings to the economy, development of other methods of macroeconomic control is imperative. One danger from the price changes brought about by reform is inflation. Reform need not carry a lasting inflationary bias, however, if government exercises appropriate control of fiscal and monetary policy--control that is intimately linked with imposing financial discipline on state enterprises. CPEs display excess demand in many markets and supply-side measures are not likely to resolve these problems in the short term; while this "overhang" is being eliminated, the government must pursue policies that maintain faith in the currency and establish real incentives for saving in financial instruments and discourage hedging against inflation by holding real commodities.

The fiscal system needs to provide a more stable and uniform tax and subsidy system, one that is less subject to negotiation and discretionary modification in response to pressure form state enterprises. Early reforms, which attempted to shift the means of control from physical targets to financial targets, suffered because of the power of state enterprises to negotiate subsidies and tax reliefs in order to achieve their targets; enterprises were interested not in their pre-tax profit (as a reflection of efficiency and innovation) but only in the after-tax result. Increased attention also needs to be directed at both reducing the scale and scope of consumer subsidies and making those subsidies more explicit. Thus, a key reform is transferring to the budget the cost of implicit subsidies given by the banking sector to state enterprise borrowing and housing finance.

Reform of the financial sector needs to move in step with fiscal reform. As the source of capital for investment is moved from the government budget to the banking system, the system needs to take up the intermediation between household savings and investment capital demand

and take a less passive, more independent role in the allocation of credit. These changes require a central bank with independence to set monetary policy and a legal framework for enforcing bankruptcy actions against defaulting borrowers. Past reforms of the financial sector have often faltered on the unwillingness to establish positive real interest rates to mobilize savings and control demand for credit.

The Reform Process to Date

The key stumbling block to greater success in the reform process has been the government's unwillingness to accept market allocation as a substitute for central planning--most have viewed the market as a facilitating instrument for improved central control over the economy. Little attention was given to how such reforms would affect the viability of state enterprises or the continuation of major social policies, such as guaranteed employment and low-cost food and housing.

This is not to say there has been no real progress. Significant changes have already been made or are under way. Most CPEs have taken steps to reduce the power of planning agencies to exert control and granted greater autonomy to state enterprises. Administrative control over some prices has been relaxed and greater transparency in the links between the domestic economy and foreign markets have been established. Greater freedom has been granted to state enterprises over wages and their workforce; steps to increase labor mobility have been attempted. A more uniform financial environment is being developed and private enterprises are less subject to discriminatory regulation. All these developments are described in detail in Part II.

The reform process is still hampered by remnants of the central planning system and its associated policies, however. Government and state enterprise bureaucracies are unwilling to give up the wide range of powers they enjoyed in the traditional CPE. Industries and sector favored under the previous CPE development strategy fear the loss of easy access to investment funds and preferential taxes and subsidies. The dislocation inherent in the restructuring of the economy represents a strong threat to households, which face the erosion of economic guarantees to employment and basic needs such as food and shelter. Finally, only recently have the governments and populations of CPEs recognized the existence of a basic trade-off between economic efficiency and living standards on one hand and economic security and income equality on the other.

Reformers are also faced with the decision about how fast to proceed. On the one hand, fast-paced reform minimizes the time required to capture the efficiency gains of structural adjustment but may cause wide swings in production and investment as residual institutional rigidities persist. Such swings could cause significant pressure for relaxing financial discipline on state enterprises, slowing the pace of reform. On the other hand, step-by-step reform, while it reduces the need for preparatory institutional reform, runs the risk of not delivering enough gains, causing the reform effort to run out of momentum. It also raises difficult questions about how to sequence the key reforms. Little is known about the "optimal" path of reform, but it may be necessary to advance reforms on a broad front once a certain stage in the reform process is reached.

The final handicap to the process of reform has been the absence of a well-defined strategy for how reform will proceed. In most cases (until very recently), reform was simply instituted in an ad hoc fashion when the combination of pressures in the economy, design of the reform, and political acceptability came together. This has produced reform programs that move with quite different speeds and are often subject to revision and retrenchment. The problem is compounded by the fact that most governments do not have a clear vision of what the "reformed" system would look like--they are committed only to change in a certain direction, but not to how far the change must be taken to achieve the level of economic performance desired. In the end, the basic decision about how closely the reformed CPEs will look like Western free-market economies will be a political trade-off between equality and security on the one hand and efficiency and higher living standards on the other.

Notes, chapter two

1. SOEs are the production units in the CPE and range in size from a single factory to large vertically and horizontally integrated conglomerates.

2. This and the following section draw mainly on the discussions of the structure and problems of CPEs in chapters 3 and 4 of Hewett (1988), chapters 4 and 5 of Harding (1987), and IMF (1989a).

3. See chapters 4 and 5 for detailed discussions of the reform process in these countries.

4. One danger of the slow pace is that "spontaneous" privatization (the unauthorized sale or takeover of an enterprise by managers), which typically undervalues the assets being sold, may overtake government efforts and reduce the return to the state (and society) on its massive investment over the past decades. Interview with David Levintow, Center for Privatization, Washington, D.C. Also, see Hinds (1990).

Chapter Three

THE COUNTRIES OF EASTERN EUROPE
IN COMPARATIVE PERSPECTIVE

This chapter provides a comparative view of the economies, housing sectors, and size (population) of the six countries covered by the report. As such it complements the individual country presentations of the following six chapters which have been written largely to be self contained.

The basic data, presented in table 3.1, are somewhat limited because many figures are not available on a comparable basis for all the countries. The table contains data for three years for each of the six countries--1980, 1985, and 1988--so that the trends in recent years are evident. In addition to the data for these countries, we have included similar data for West Germany to provide a contrast with the situation in a nearby market-oriented economy.

POPULATION AND URBANIZATION

In terms of population the six countries fall into two groups: three smaller countries--Bulgaria, Czechoslovakia, and Hungary--with 1988 populations of 9.0 to 15.6 million; and three larger countries, with 1988 populations ranging from 23.1 million in Romania to 37.9 million in Poland. Overall population growth rates are universally low, at under 1 percent a year. The degree and pace of urbanization also varies. In Romania and Yugoslavia about half the people are urban dwellers, and this share has remained fairly constant during the 1980s. At the other end of the spectrum, in Czechoslovakia 76 percent of the population lives in urban areas, sharply up from its 62 percent in 1980. Urbanization in Bulgaria, Hungary, and Poland is about 60 percent, with modest increases in the 1980s. For reference, urbanization in West Germany was 86 percent in 1988.

ECONOMIC PERFORMANCE

Perhaps the most comprehensive measure of sustained economic performance is the rough equivalent of GNP per capita in centrally planned economies, Net Material Product (NMP) per capita.[1] By far the highest level of well-being among Eastern European countries as indicated by this measure is enjoyed by Czechoslovakia; in 1988 NMP per capita was $7,198 when valued at the official exchange rate.[2] This figure is 78 percent greater than Bulgaria's $4,036, which ranks second among these countries. However, it is only slightly more than half of West Germany's per capita output--$13,217. Poland recorded the lowest NMP per capita among in 1988, at $1,533, with Romania ($2,491) and Yugoslavia ($2,153) not far above it.

The transition to market-oriented economies for these countries is proving difficult. The UN Economic Commission for Europe reports that in 1989 the economies of these countries performed poorly, and a deepening recession

Table 3.1   SUMMARY DATA--EASTERN EUROPE 1980-88

	Bulgaria		
	1980	1985	1988
Population			
Total (millions)[a]	8.9	9.0	9.0
Annual growth (percent)[a]	0.3	**	0.1
Urban share (percent)[b]	62.2	65.5	66.7
National income and investment			
NMP (billion dollars)[c,d]	13.3	24.3	36.2
Annual NMP growth (percent)[e]	5.7	2.2	-0.4
GFCF (percent of NMP)[e]	..	34.5	34.6
Per capita NMP (dollars)	1,504	2,711	4,036
External balance (billion dollars)[e,f]			
Exports	3.1	3.1	2.7
Imports	2.1	3.1	3.9
Current account	1.0	-0.2	-1.2
Gross external debt	3.5	3.6	7.6
Housing sector[h]			
stock (million units)[a]	2.8	3.2	3.3
Average inhabitants per unit			
(persons)	3.1	2.8	2.7
Floor space per capita (sq. meters)[a]	18.9	22.9	25.3
Gross production (thous. units)[a]	74.3	64.9	63.0
Gross production per 1,000			
inhabitants (units)	8.4	7.2	7.0
Investment (percent of NMP)[g]	4.6	4.4	..
Share of gross production			
(as investors): (percent)[a]			
State and SOEs	52.0	46.4	47.1
Cooperatives	24.1	26.0	20.2
Private individuals	24.0	27.6	32.7

Table 3.1   *Continued*

	Czechoslovakia		
	1980	1985	1988
Population			
Total (millions)[a]	15.3	15.5	15.6
Annual growth (percent)[a]	0.3	0.3	0.3
Urban share (percent)[b]	62.3	74.7	76.0
National income and investment			
NMP (billion dollars)[c,d]	86.2	80.0	112.4
Annual NMP growth (percent)[e]	2.9	3.0	2.9
GFCF (percent of NMP)[e]	30.0	32.9	..
Per capita NMP (dollars)	5,628	5,161	7,198
External balance (billion dollars)[e,f]			
Exports	4.5	4.0	5.1
Imports	4.5	3.4	5.2
Current account	-0.4	0.5	0.3
Gross external debt	4.9	3.6	5.3
Housing sector[h]			
stock (million units)[a]	5.3	5.7	5.9
Average inhabitants per unit			
(persons)	2.9	2.7	2.7
Floor space per capita (sq. meters)[a]	26.3	29.3	30.9
Gross production (thous. units)[a]	128.8	104.4	82.9
Gross production per 1,000			
inhabitants (units)	8.4	6.7	5.3
Investment (percent of NMP)[g]	4.4	3.7	..
Share of gross production			
(as investors): (percent)[a]			
State and SOEs	38.8	23.1	28.4
Cooperatives	37.0	50.5	44.5
Private individuals	24.2	26.3	27.1

	Hungary			Poland	
1980	1985	1988	1980	1985	1988
10.7	10.6	10.6	35.6	37.2	37.9
**	**	**	0.8	0.8	0.5
53.5	56.6	59.3	58.4	60.1	61.2
17.9	16.8	23.0	45.0	58.4	58.0
0.2	-1.2	5.4	-8.1	3.4	4.9
21.9	27.6	30.3	31.2	25.8	26.7
1,673	1,580	2,170	1,266	1,569	1,533
4.9	4.5	5.9	8.0	6.1	8.3
4.6	4.9	5.3	8.7	5.1	7.2
-0.4	-0.5	-0.6	-2.6	-0.8	-0.6
9.1	11.8	17.3	25.1	29.3	39.2
3.8	3.8	4.0	9.8	10.7	10.8
2.8	2.8	2.7	3.6	3.5	3.5
23.6	28.5	31.9	17.6	19.9	21.1
89.1	69.4	50.6	217.1	189.6	189.6
8.3	6.5	4.8	6.1	5.1	5.0
6.8	5.4	..	6.8	6.1	..
34.1	17.9	10.3	18.2	22.4	20.9
4.7	3.3	1.8	56.2	47.7	45.3
61.2	78.8	87.9	25.7	29.9	33.8

Table 3.1　*(Continued)*

	Romania		
	1980	1985	1988
Population Total (millions)[a]	22.2	22.7	23.1
Annual growth (percent)[a]	0.6	0.3	0.4
Urban share (percent)[b]	49.6	49.0	49.7
National income and investment			
NMP (billion dollars)[c,d]	31.1	43.8	57.6
Annual NMP growth (percent)[e]	3.3	-0.4	3.2
GFCF (percent of NMP)[e]	38.0	34.1	..
Per capita NMP (dollars)	1,400	1,929	2,491
External balance (billion dollars)[e,f]			
Exports	6.5	6.3	6.6
Imports	8.0	4.8	4.1
Current account	-2.4	0.9	2.3
Gross external debt	9.4	6.6	3.5
Housing sector[h]			
stock (million units)[a]	..	..	..
Average inhabitants per unit (persons)	..	..	..
Floor space per capita (sq. meters)[a]	..	..	..
Gross production (thous. units)[a]	197.8	105.6	..
Gross production per 1,000 inhabitants (units)	8.9	4.6	..
Investment (percent of NMP)[g]	4.3	2.3	..
Share of gross production (as investors): (percent)[a]			
State and SOEs	94.3	91.8	..
Cooperatives	..	..	..
Private individuals	..	..	..

	Yugoslavia			West Germany		
	1980	1985	1988	1980	1985	1988
	22.3	23.1	23.6	61.6	61.0	61.2
	0.6	0.7	0.6	0.2	-0.3	**
	42.3	46.5	..	84.4	85.5	86.2
	63.1	41.7	50.7	813.6	621.8	1,202.0
	2.3	1.5	-1.5	**	1.9	3.4
	35.1	20.5	19.4	21.7	19.7	19.9
	2,831	1,805	2,153	13,217	10,190	19,640
	5.7	6.5	9.4	234.0	223.8	395.3
	11.3	7.7	10.1	234.9	196.9	328.6
	-2.2	0.9	2.2	-13.9	17.0	48.6
	17.4	18.8	18.7	20.9	36.0	..
	6.3	6.8	7.0	25.4	27.1	27.7
	3.5	3.4	3.4	2.4	2.3	2.2
	20.1	21.3	21.9	41.9	39.8	44.9
	136.8	127.6	120.3	452.3	387.2	208.6
	6.1	5.5	5.1	7.3	6.3	3.4
	..	..	..	7.1	5.6	5.3
	35.6	33.5	31.7	1.3	1.2	1.6
	..	..	..	15.6	6.4	5.8
	..	..	..	83.1	92.4	92.5

Notes, table 3.1

..   No data available
**   Negligible (less than 0.05)
a.   United Nations (1989)
b.   Romania: United Nations (1986)
c.   Output valued at official commercial exchange rate
d.   Yugoslav output is Gross Social Product (GSP); GSP = NMP + capital consumption; West German output is GDP.
e.   EIU (various)
f.   Convertible currencies only
g.   United Nations (1988)
h.   Data for Yugoslavia are for 1980, 1985, and 1987

expected for 1990. The Yugoslav and Polish economies were particularly battered in 1989 and 1990 by the aftermath of inflationary spirals. Poland's January 1990 shock therapy of price liberalization and wage freeze stopped inflation, but at the cost of a sharp reduction in output. Yugoslavia has faced a similar squeeze in output as price rises have been curbed by limits on central bank credit expansion and fixing the exchange rate of the dinar to the Deutschemark.

Future growth depends on the extent of current and past investment in the national economy. Table 3.1 shows Gross Fixed Capital Formation (GFCF) as a percent of NMP. The overall rates for the Eastern European countries are high compared to West Germany's 20 percent; but their overall capital stock per employee is much smaller. Among the Eastern European countries, four devoted 30 percent or more to investment in the most recent year for which we have data--Romania, Bulgaria, Czechoslovakia, and Hungary. Among these, only Hungary shows a clear increase in the percentage of NMP going to GFCF during the 1980s. Poland and Yugoslavia had lower rates of investment in 1988, rates which had declined significantly in the 1980s, reflecting the turbulence in both economies. A critical input for economic reform in the years ahead will be importation of western technology and capital goods which can make production competitive in the world market. The ability to import depends, in part, on the volume of external debt a country has accumulated: the larger its debt, the larger the share of its hard currency earnings must go to pay foreign creditors rather than financing imports. Table 3.1 provides basic data on the balance of payments position (for trade conducted in convertible currencies). Table 3.2 presents two additional data items for 1988 which are easier to interpret: per capita gross external debt and the ratio of gross external debt to exports. The two items should be read together, since gross external debt is easier to manage when exports are high and the current account balance is positive.

These figures make clear the relatively difficult positions of Poland, Yugoslavia, and Hungary. All have high absolute gross external debt positions on a per capita basis and high debt relative to exports. Among the three, Poland and Hungary have consistently run a current account deficit; Yugoslavia has had a stronger current account position, in part due to overseas workers' remittances. In contrast Czechoslovakia and Romania have small gross debts and low ratios of debt to exports, although Romania's favorable position was achieved only through truly draconian measures (see chapter 9).

THE HOUSING SECTOR

Three aspects the housing sectors in Eastern European countries are discussed in this section. First, we examine

Table 3.2   EASTERN EUROPE DEBT INDICATORS 1988

	Per Capita Gross External Debt (dollars)	Gross External Debt/Exports
Bulgaria	844	2.8
Czechoslovakia	340	1.0
Hungary	1,632	2.7
Poland	1,034	4.7
Romania	149	0.5
Yugoslavia	792	2.0
West Germany	590	0.2

Source: Table 3.1

how well the population is housed, using a couple of key measures that are widely available. Second, we discuss housing production in the 1980s. Finally, we turn to the allocation of new housing production among the state, cooperatives, and private individuals.

Housing Occupancy

All these Eastern European countries suffer from housing shortages, which are heavily concentrated in urban areas. In Part II we present various data measuring the shortfall between household formations and the production of new units. Here we focus on two indicators--the average number of inhabitants per unit and floor space per capita (in square meters).

The contrast between the six Eastern European countries under study and West Germany is striking. The six countries have an (unweighted) average of 3.0 persons per unit--36 percent more than in West Germany--and 26.2 square meters of floor space per capita--only 58 percent of West Germany's.[3]

On these measures, as on others, Poland and Yugoslavia are much worse off than the other Eastern European countries with impressively more inhabitants per dwelling--about 3.5 versus 2.7--*and* sharply fewer square meters per person--about 21.5 versus an average of about 29.3.[4] Moreover, there has been little improvement in space per person in Poland and Yugoslavia during the 1980s, in contrast to substantial increases for the other countries. In Bulgaria, for example, space per person rose from 18.9 to 25.3 square meters between 1980 and 1988.

Housing Production

In all six countries in Eastern Europe, the number of units built per 1,000 population declined during the 1980s. In 1980 housing output ranged between 8.9 and 6.1 units per 1,000 persons, with four countries with over 8.0 units per 1,000; by 1988 the range had dropped to between 7.0 and 4.6, with only one country (Bulgaria) over 5.3 units per 1,000 persons. Thus, housing markets are becoming increasingly tight, with a rising share of households doubled up, usually in the form of young couples living with one of their parents.[5]

While the available data on the share of NMP accounted for by housing investment are not as complete as on the number of units produced, the figures we have suggest that investment has not declined as much as the number of new units produced. This is accounted for in part by improvements in the quality and size of the new units constructed, i.e., more investment per unit. However, as discussed in detail in Part II, it is partly attributable to declines in the productivity of the state owned enterprises (SOEs), which have typically been responsible for the majority of production in these countries.

Housing Demand

The composition of clients for new housing changed during the 1980s. The state and SOEs are the clients for new social housing and for housing to be allocated by the SOEs to their workers; nearly all such housing is built by state construction enterprises. In contrast, housing destined for occupancy by members of cooperatives is constructed by both the cooperatives themselves and SOEs, with the majority apparently in the latter category.[6] Lastly, housing purchased by private individuals is generally built by small contractors or literally by the family itself; most of this housing is being built outside the largest cities.

In the four countries (Bulgaria, Czechoslovakia, Hungary, and Poland) for which we have data for both 1980 and 1988, the trend is clear. Production for private purchase rose in all four, and on average from 34 to 46 percent (see table 3.3). Within the averages, however, there is substantial diversity. In Hungary in 1988, nearly 90 percent of new units were for private individuals, much of it built through self-help efforts. In Poland, in contrast, cooperatives accounted for the largest share of output, 45 percent in 1988. State production declined by only 5 percentage points in Bulgaria with the share of state production actually increased marginally during the period 1985 to 1988 after a large fall between 1980 and 1985. In Romania, which is not included in the average shown in table 3.3, over 90 percent of units are still being constructed by the state and SOEs. State production in Yugo-

Table 3.3   EASTERN EUROPE HOUSING INVESTORS
1980-88 (percent of total units produced)

	1980	1988
State and SOEs	35.8	28.5
Cooperatives	30.2	28.0
Private individuals	33.8	45.5

Source: Table 3.1.

Note: These are unweighted averages for four countries (Bulgaria, Czechoslovakia, Hungary, and Poland).

slavia has declined since 1980, but no data is available to indicate how the difference has been made up between cooperatives and private investors.

These data are a strong signal that individual families are finding ways to substitute for the declining role of the state in most of these countries. Still, as discussed later, the impediments to private production generally remain formidable. One of the challenges to the governments of these countries will be to level the housing construction playing field.

Notes, chapter three

1. NMP is defined in note 2 in chapter 1.

2. Because most of the countries of Eastern Europe have allowed their official exchange rate to be seriously overvalued for extended periods, the NMP figures shown can be overstated. Trends in NMP are particularly difficult to interpret because of episodic currency revaluations.

3. West Germany's housing situation (while certainly good) is not nearly as favorable as that in the United States, for example. For details, see Stahl and Struyk (1985), chapter 1.

4. The comparison group of countries excludes Romania for which these data are not available.

5. Output in West Germany also declined very sharply during the 1980s. However, in this case production was curtailed because the housing shortage dating from the World War II was finally completely eliminated and the number of new households forming had settled at a lower level. This situation was dramatically reversed in 1989 with the massive influx of Germans from East European countries and the government took steps to encourage additional production (Lammerskitten 1990).

6. Cooperatives are associations of individuals which form to provide their members with housing. They take different forms in different countries, acting as investors and as construction contractors in some countries, solely as investors in others.

Chapter Four

THE HOUSING SECTOR IN HUNGARY

For 20 years Hungary has experimented with piecemeal reforms aimed at reducing the rigidities inherent in a command-driven economy. At each step in the process the removal of one constraint has led to recognition of another layer of constraints. As a result, the history of Hungary's reform experience since 1968 is replete with small successes and frustrating setbacks, of formal controls and directives from the center being gradually relinquished and then new measures being introduced to ensure indirect control.

One of the paradoxes of this chipping away process is that although it appeared to succeed in creating conditions of macroeconomic stabilization between 1968 and 1986, it did not create the basis for sustained economic growth (IMF 1989b). Although corrections were introduced at the macro level of the economy, they tended not to be deep, systemic reforms. Correspondingly, instead of stimulating the economy, microeconomic policies tended to act as a brake on growth.[1]

DEMOGRAPHIC TRENDS

Hungary is a small country of 10.7 million people. A homogeneous country, Hungary has avoided the strife of multi-ethnic countries such as Yugoslavia and Bulgaria. Several demographic trends are of particular interest:

- After falling in the exodus years after the 1956 revolution, population rose slowly during the 1960s and 1970s, stabilized during the 1980s, and is expected to rise slightly throughout the 1990s (see table 4.1).

- Hungary has a rapidly aging population: currently, for every two persons employed, one person is retired and receives a pension. The dependency ratio remains stable, however, because of the declining share of children in the total population.

- In 1980, the last census year, there were about 3.7 million households, of which 2.7 million were single-family households and 700,000 one-person households. The number of households is increasing at a higher rate than the population as a whole, however, so the demand for housing is increasing faster than the rate of population growth would indicate.

- About 59 percent of the population lived in urban areas in 1988; in 1960 the figure was 39.3 percent.

- Of the 30 percent of the population in the 9 largest cities, 19 percent or 2.1 million live in Budapest; with the next largest city (Miskoic) at 220,000, Hungary clearly reflects the old urban settlement pattern of the dominant central city.

Table 4.1   HUNGARY -- POPULATION TRENDS 1970-2000

	1970	1980	1990	2000
Total population (millions)	10.4	10.7	10.7	10.7
Percent of total				
Age 14 and under	20.8	21.9	20.2	18.4
Age 15-64	67.6	64.6	66.3	66.7
Age 65 and over	11.5	13.4	13.5	14.4
Dependency ratio[a] (percent)	47.8	54.7	50.7	49.9
Urban population (percent)	45.6	53.5	58.9	62.9
Annual growth (percent)				
Total	0.4	0.3	-0.1	0.1
Urban	1.7	1.6	0.9	0.7
Rural	-0.7	-1.1	-1.3	-0.9

Source: United Nations (1986).

a. The dependency ratio is the sum of the population under age 15 and age 65 and over divided by the population age 15-64 expressed as a percentage.

ECONOMIC OVERVIEW

We begin with a summary of reforms to the economy as a whole to establish the context for developments in the housing sector. In particular, we focus on reforms that affect state enterprises and the private sector, the financial sector, and the control of wages and prices. Reform in these areas is key to the development of the housing sector.

State Enterprises

Up until 1968 and the introduction of the New Economic Mechanism (NEM)--Hungary's first effort at market reform--the economy was patterned on the classic principles of a centralized system of planning. The NEM, radical in its time, attempted to modify management of the economy by eliminating plan directives from the center and permitting greater enterprise autonomy in planning, production, and pricing. Decision-making power, which had been vested exclusively in supervisory agencies--ministries or local authorities--and used to set physical output targets and allocate materials for production, was modestly decentralized. However, measures to retain indirect control were implemented concurrently. The practical result was that state enterprises bargained back and forth with the authorities for preferential treatment in the application of the instruments of indirect control: credits, subsidies, and tax exemptions. In fact, the bargaining process acted as a disincentive to any real financial discipline and the notion of pretax profitability as an indicator of performance was virtually ignored. This pattern of operation continued for nearly 10 years.

The reform process picked up again in 1977 and has continued ever since. A number of important laws, acts, and measures were implemented over this period. We summarize those most germane to the evolution of state enterprises:[2]

State Enterprise Act of 1977. With amendments in 1981 and 1982, and related legislation effective in 1985, this law was intended to decentralize decisionmaking in state enterprises, relying on self-management with worker participation. But with macroeconomic imbalances becoming an increasing source of concern in 1986, tax-based wage controls were tightened and controls by central authorities on price adjustments were enforced more strictly, undercutting enterprise autonomy and discipline.

Bankruptcy Law of 1986. This law was intended to facilitate the restructuring or liquidation of inefficient enterprises. State subsidy payments to creditors that failed to enforce the collection of overdue claims were stopped, and tax forgiveness to loss-makers discontinued. But insolvent enterprises were allowed to opt for reflotation with government support instead of bankruptcy, and creditors were reluctant to initiate bankruptcy proceedings against large, chronic loss-makers that may be their principal or sole customers. Through 1989, most proceedings were initiated by the insolvent enterprises themselves. The year 1990 has seen greater activity, with a bankruptcy suit brought against the national bus manufacturer in March and plans by government to close about 20 of the worst loss-making state enterprises in the second half of the year.

National Property Agency (NPA). Legislation was passed in January 1990 establishing the NPA to facilitate privatization and regulations to ensure that the interests of the state, as owner-seller, are protected, both from the point of view of national policy interests and avoidance of bargain transfers wherever possible. One role envisioned by advisors to the NPA is that it will help develop Hungary's capital market through the sale of shares and bonds to the public, to financial institutions, and to mutual funds that will lead to secondary market activity. It is likely that the government will permit "spontaneous privatization" (selling off of state-owned assets by management and workers' councils in self-governing enterprises at a fraction of their value) to continue but will place limits on the "dumping" that has been occurring (Tomlinson 1990).[3]

Of the 2,700 state-owned enterprises (SOEs) in Hungary, constituting 90 percent of all enterprises in the country, the top 20 percent, or 540, will be the focus of the NPA. Of all SOEs, 80 percent are run by employee-managed councils in which management and workers jointly hold shares in the company. In the past, some 1,800 laws have governed SOEs in Hungary. Close to 1,000 reportedly have been repealed (Levintow 1990).

Private Sector

As a result of the postwar policy of industrialization in Hungary, most enterprises underwent mergers to facilitate central control and to promote large-scale production. Few small- and medium-sized enterprises (SMSEs) survived. Just ten years ago, in 1980, the IMF estimated that "the share of industrial employment in enterprises of up to 50 employees, which is about 15 percent in market economies, was only 0.1 percent in Hungary" (IMF 1989b).

During the 1980s, however, Hungary took a number of progressive steps to open up the economy and promote greater competition. Although initial efforts focused on nurturing the creation of small and medium-sized enterprises in the socialized sector, other efforts supported the growth of small-scale cooperative associations. By the end of 1986, some 35,000 new, small enterprises with 440,000 employees (about 9 percent of the labor force) had been created. By 1987, "the share of incomes earned in the private sector [totalled] 20.5 percent of household disposable income" (IMF 1989b). While this was encouraging, numerous restrictions continued to hamper the development of a competitive private sector. However, significant improvements have been registered recently in three areas. First, the Corporate Association Law in 1989 permitted both private residents and nonresidents to establish a variety of enterprise forms, including unlimited liability companies and joint ventures with a limited liability, as well as joint stock companies. Second, private businesses may now employ up to 500 workers, usually considered the threshold level for a medium-sized firm. And third, beginning in 1989, a number of new initiatives were introduced to facilitate trade and foreign investment.[4]

During 1987, 24 new share corporations, including 8 banks, were established in Hungary, and in 1988 an additional 89 new share corporations were set up. By mid-1989, 16 countries had participated in about 280 joint ventures in Hungary. Two foreign investment funds, the First Hungary Fund Limited and the Hungarian Investment Company, have been established to help finance joint venture projects, privatization efforts, and provide venture capital for start-up companies. In June, a stock exchange opened in Budapest and it is expected that about a dozen enterprises will be listed by the end of 1990. Unlike the previous stock exchange, the new institution is regulated (by the Act on Securities and Stock Exchange) and requires all listed companies to file full financial disclosures.

Two major clouds hang over this encouraging investment climate. One is Hungary's foreign debt, which at the end of 1989 totalled $20 billion. Hungary's record to date is good; it negotiated a stand-by agreement with the IMF in March and has not defaulted, been in arrears, or rescheduled any of its debt obligations. However, it is facing a heavy repayment burden: annual interest payments of $1.3 billion currently represent 4 percent of GDP; the debt service ratio, on a convertible export basis, is expected to reach 40 to 50 percent in 1990 (Komaromi 1990). The second hazard facing investors is the currency risk associated with the nonconvertibility of the forint (the government's target for convertability is between the end of 1991 and mid-1992) and its steady devaluation relative to convertible currencies. Since 1985, when the exchange rate was Ft9.7 = $1.00, the forint has lost 26 percent of its value against the dollar in the official market and about 50 percent of its value in the black market.

Financial System in Hungary

The 1968 reforms in Hungary excluded the banking sector. As a result, the banking system continued to operate with a monopolistic, highly specialized and segmented structure. The major features of this system prior to the major banking reform of 1987 can be summarized as follows:

- The National Bank of Hungary (NBH) maintained central control over the flow of capital in the country. It kept all the accounts of the state enterprises, allocated credit to them at the request of the supervisory agencies, and managed nearly all the foreign currency operations.

- The National Savings Bank (OTP), supplemented by the postal savings network and the savings cooperatives, acted as the banker of the population and local authorities. It collected deposits at low interest rates, most of which were re-lent at even lower (3 percent) rates for housing.

- A number of small financial institutions designed to finance innovations and to pool capital for selected state-controlled developments were established in the early 1980s.

- Savings Cooperatives operated only in rural areas and small towns, were limited in the forms of deposits they could accept and were not permitted to extend credit to the private sector.

- The State Insurance Company monopolized the Hungarian insurance market.

- Available savings instruments were limited to life insurance policies with the State Insurance Company, small amounts of bonds issued in 1983, coop share certificates, and real estate.

- The propensity to save was discouraged by: (1) guaranteed lifetime employment; (2) negative real interest rates on savings deposits; and (3) availability of heavily subsidized housing loans.

In an effort aimed at strengthening enterprise autonomy, stimulating savings, and introducing competition among profit-oriented commercial banks, the government, beginning in 1985, initiated a number of far-reaching reforms in the banking sector. The most important of these, which set the stage for fundamental restructuring of housing finance, are summarized below.

Commercial banking. In 1987 the National Bank of Hungary, while retaining its central bank functions, transferred its commercial activities to three new commercial banks set up as joint stock companies owned directly by the state. All the current accounts of state enterprises and cooperatives were distributed among the banks with the objective to instill profit-oriented credit-granting behavior into commercial bank practice. The banks were also free to set loan rates to enterprises, although the average charged could not exceed the refinancing rate of the NBH by more than 1.5 percent (IMF 1989b).

In addition, the dozen or so small financial institutions created in the early 1980s that operated as innovation or investment project funds have been transformed into commercial banks.

Despite the reforms just enumerated, several problems have become apparent: (1) management and technical skills needed to assess credit risk are noticeably absent; (2) the banks have been reluctant to cut off lending to inefficient enterprises; (3) consumer lending is only just beginning; and (4) there appears to be little in the way of policy or incentives to lend to private sector SMSEs (e.g., there is little evidence that commercial banks are making construction period financing available to small builders [Friedlander 1988; World Bank 1989c; Winchester 1990]).

Savings cooperatives. In 1985 the Savings Cooperatives, of which there are presently 262 with a total membership of 1.8 million, were permitted to offer banking services similar to the National Savings Bank (OTP). Small public and private enterprises were allowed to transfer their accounts from OTP to the savings coops in order to facilitate their transactions with the state enterprise sector.

Other developments. Other changes in the structure of the financial system include:

- As of July 1986, any agent of the enterprise sector can establish an insurance company, including one with foreign participation. Several have done so. The State Insurance Agency retains a monopoly for export insurance and obligatory auto collision insurance.

- Two foreign banks with foreign participation are now in operation: the Central-European International Bank Ltd., an off-shore trading company; and Citibank Budapest Rt. which began operations in 1986.

Two key reforms in the housing finance system in 1989 effectively ended the historical segmentation between commercial and savings banks. First, the granting of housing loans at low (3 percent) rates of interest was discontinued, ending OTP's virtual monopoly on mortgage lending and greatly reducing the interest rate subsidies. Second, the large stock of these concessional loans outstanding was transferred to a newly established Housing Fund in exchange for bonds with market-related yields. The losses of the Fund were covered by budget transfers (IMF 1989b; World Bank 1989b). Under these conditions commercial banks could be permitted to compete with the savings banks for deposits and for consumer lending business.

The major banks in Hungary and their key functions are presented in table 4.2.

Currently available savings instruments. The current rate on one-year time deposits is about 19 percent (net of a 20 percent withholding tax), raised from 13.5 percent in early 1990. With current inflation at about 20 percent, the interest rates offer little incentive to save.

Treasury bills are bought by both households and enterprises and banks. Households pay a fixed rate (comparable to the deposit rate at the OTP, which is lower than the deposit rate at the commercial banks.) Raised in early 1990, a 9-month T-Bill currently pays an annual rate of 19 percent (after tax). T-Bills sold at auction to enterprises and banks are zero-coupon bills. The cost of these funds to the government is significantly higher than the fixed-rate bills. For instance, the February 8 rate was 26 percent (Winchester 1990).

Some commercial banks are competing very actively with OTP for household savings. One bank, for example, has introduced 3- and 6-month CDs. In general, though, the volume of funds brought into the commercial banks is still low. One banker attributes this to the fact that many households have large housing loan debts to OTP which, combined with inflation, are soaking up excess liquidity (Winchester 1990).

The issuance of bonds was resumed in 1981 after a hiatus of 30 years, first by local councils to finance infrastructure, and since 1983 also by state enterprises. Volume declined in 1988, however, because of four factors: (1) government guarantees for bonds were discontinued in early 1987; (2) enterprises and banks were anticipating increased inflation, which would make fixed-rate bonds unattractive; (3) competition from T-Bills and CDs increased in early 1988; and (4) there is no reliable accounting information on the enterprises and banks to evaluate their creditworthiness as debtors.

Apart from the insurance companies, plans are underway to establish brokerage houses to operate in the newly-formed stock exchange. At the current time, there are no pension funds, though there is a large block of trust funds comprising all the state-controlled pensions.

Table 4.2 FINANCIAL INSTITUTIONS IN HUNGARY

English Name	Magyar Acronym	Year Founded	Capitalization (Ft million)	Ownership	Chief Functions
National Bank of Hungary	MNB	1924	1,500	State Owned	Central Bank (monetary authority, supervises commercial banks, sets interest rates)
AGROBANK	A	1984	1,500	Joint Stock (100% coops)	Agriculture and food processing finance (coops and private firms)
Budapest Bank Ltd.	BHB	1986	6,400	Joint Stock (61% state)	Small- and medium-sized business finance (coop and private firms)
Commercial & Credit Bank Ltd.	K&H	1987	10,600	Joint Stock (50% state)	Joint venture financing
Hungarian Credit Bank	MHB	1987	14,000	Joint Stock (100% coop and firms)	Short-term trade credit, construction, and mortgage financing

(continued)

Table 4.2   (Continued)

English Name	Magyar Acronym	Year Founded	Capitalization (Ft million)	Ownership	Chief Functions
Hungarian Foreign Trade Bank Ltd.	MKB	1980	6,000	State Owned	Foreign trade and currency
Innovation Bank for Construction Ind.	EIB	1983	1,200	Joint Stock (firms and banks)	Commerical, industrial, construction, and real estate financing; property management
INTERBANK for Foreign Trade Ltd.	I	1980 (private 1988)	2,200	Joint Stock (trade firms and coops)	Development financing for export/import
General Banking & Trust Co. Ltd.		1952 (private 1986)	1,500	Joint Stock	
General Bank for Ventura Financing Ltd.		1965	2,200		

MEZOBANK National Banking Inst. of Agi Co-ops Co. Ltd.	MB	1986	2,000	Joint Stock (coops)	Agricultural cooperative financing
National Savings Bank	OPT	1988	1,300	State Owned	Residential real estate (construction, marketing, and financing)
Post Bank	PB	1988	2,200	State Owned	Collection of deposits, loans to other banks
Savings Cooperatives	T	1957	10,000	State Owned	Analogous to U.S. credit unions
Real Estate Bank Ltd.		Being formed		Joint Stock	Formerly subsidiary of MHB for real estate brokering, development, and finance

Source: Parry (1989).

Wages, the "Second Economy," and Prices

Wage policy in the pre-1968 period was driven by the ideological tenets of socialism. Food, shelter, health care, education, and transport were viewed as social rights and provided to every citizen at heavily subsidized prices. Wages were not intended to reflect the cost or scarcity of labor. However, central planning judgments on compensation were supplemented with consumer price subsidies and social benefits in money and kind, much of which was financed by heavy taxes levied on enterprises.

Successive reforms of the wage system were introduced in 1968, 1976, 1980, 1983, 1985, and 1988. Each reflected an effort to allow for a differentiation of wages to permit payment of better incentives for performance, and in 1985 to stimulate labor mobility. Some used complex schemes to regulate wages through enterprise taxation. In 1988 a personal income tax was introduced, along with a 50 percent corporate profit tax on wage increases. In every case, though, these schemes were not based on a real policy of deregulation but rather on controlling inflationary tendencies. They were enormously complex to implement and administratively onerous for state and local authorities as well as for the enterprises themselves.

The low and undifferentiated wage structure, together with the gradual reduction of retail price subsidies, accelerated the pace at which workers entered the "second economy." It is not unusual today for a Hungarian worker to hold two or even three jobs. Second-economy earnings are reported to be considerably higher than enterprise sector wages, which today average the equivalent of $140 per month. The result has been the informal creation of two income classes: one that is completely dependent on first-economy wages and another that enjoys combined income from first and second economies. The differential purchasing power of the two income classes is having a significant effect on household ability to buy goods and services in Hungary today, an ability that is especially startling in the housing sector.

Price reforms were an integral part of the 1968 economic reform effort, as well as subsequent efforts throughout the 1970s and 1980s to experiment with the use of market signals to producers and consumers. However, indirect administrative controls and special fiscal instruments, such as taxes, tax exemptions, and subsidies, had a dampening effect on these experiments. Nevertheless, Hungary was able to avoid the major distortions to relative prices that are a common feature of most CPEs.

Through this gradual lifting of price controls, by 1989 about 60 percent of prices were set "freely" in the Hungarian economy (IMF 1989b). In 1990, prices on many heavily subsidized commodities and public services, such as residential rents, transport, telephones, water, and sewerage, have been raised dramatically in a series of increases as part of the stand-by agreement with the IMF.

THE HOUSING SECTOR IN HUNGARY

Not surprisingly, Hungary's housing policies over the last 40 years have reflected the rhythm of its broader economic policies. In the 1960s housing was enshrined as an entitlement. A broad array of administrative powers was exercised by the state to control housing investment as well as the allocation and pricing of housing. In response to unintended and disappointing effects of public policy, various corrective measures were introduced in 1971, 1983, and 1989 to stimulate production and reduce inefficiencies and inequalities that had arisen. Partial reform measures induced partial performance improvements. Market mechanisms have been tinkered with but not fully embraced. Nevertheless, there has been an overall movement toward market-driven operations in the sector.

Overall, Hungary's housing sector has performed quite well in comparison to other Eastern European countries. By 1987, the share of housing investment in total state investment outlays reached 19 percent and housing investment as a share of GDP has remained steady at close to 6 percent (Matras 1989).

Today 90 percent of all new housing being produced in Hungary is for private ownership and only 10 percent for state ownership. However, the state still owns approximately 25 percent of all the dwelling units, including 60 percent of the stock in Budapest and 30 percent in the other towns. Although Hungary's homeownership rate stands at a remarkably high 75 percent, its growth in urban areas, especially Budapest, has been impeded by policies favoring the production of heavily subsidized rental units. In Budapest, only about 34 percent of households own their units compared with 66 percent in the towns (settlements with more than 8,000 people), and 92 percent in the villages (Sillince 1985).

Housing Stock and Production

It may be useful to start with a definition of housing types found in Hungary and a schema (see figure 4.1) that depicts Hungary's complex housing delivery system (Baross 1987).

Under the public sector delivery system three housing types are found:

Figure 4.1   HOUSING DELIVERY SYSTEM IN HUNGARY

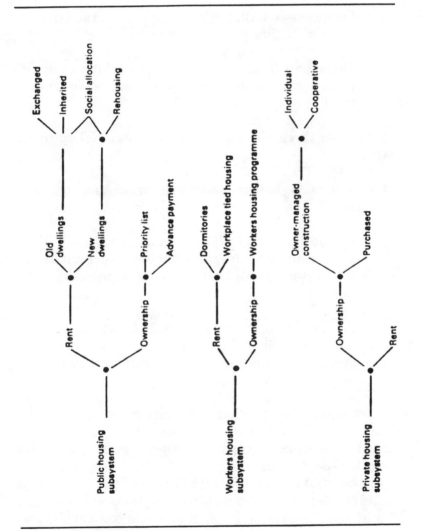

Source: Baross (1987).

- Apartments (nationalized, old upper-class 3-5 storey buildings in central locations);

- Flats (newly built high-rise blocks on the outskirts of the city);

- Tenements (nationalized former working-class rental units, usually with common service provision).

Another three housing types are found in the private sector:

- Villas (single-family houses in prestigious locations);

- Condominiums (modern, newly-constructed private apartments, generally low-rise, built as in-fill projects replacing war-damaged buildings);

- Family houses (newly-constructed single-family dwellings built in the outer suburbs where infrastructure and related services may or may not exist).

Who gets access to which housing class at what cost has been one of the most enduring questions in Hungary, one that has produced a startling range of policy responses over the last 30 years.

In contrast to structure types in the public and private sectors, there are three major subsystems in Hungary's housing delivery system, each of which has a rental and ownership element (see figure 4.1):

- Public housing (government produced and allocated);

- Worker housing (tied to enterprise employment);

  Private housing (mostly families who either individually or in small cooperatives finance the construction of their houses).

Some of the subsystems overlap. For example, some of the new units produced by the municipal authorities (local councils) are sold to individual families and end up in the private housing subsystem. In addition, households who live in municipal housing engage in a number of different private transactions, such as exchange, co-renting, and sub-renting.

Planning, Land, and Infrastructure

The government responded to the immense inequalities and scarcities at the end of World War II by: (1) redistributing the existing housing stock; and (2) establishing state enterprises to construct housing and operate the rental housing sector. Both the nationalized existing flats as well as newly built ones were allocated on the basis of need.

Planning in the socialized sector was performed by state authorities, who also approved individual projects. Implementation was the function of the local council. During the period of heavy industrialization in the 1950s, the state concentrated on building flats in the new industrial areas of the north. By 1960, however, the number of households exceeded the number of dwellings by 16 percent. These chronic shortages induced the government in 1960 to launch the First 15-Year Housing Plan (1960-1975) aimed at constructing 1 million new units. Planning authority became highly centralized. It was decreed that 60 percent of the new units be built in the capital and industrial areas, 60 percent by the state, and 40 percent by private sources. The Ministry of Construction determined the number of new units to be constructed, the number of rooms, types of amenities, and the construction technology employed. Although the plan target was met and even exceeded by 50,000 units, the net addition was less over the 15 years because of the demolition of 230,000 units. Of all units built over this 15-year period, only 36 percent were built directly by the state.

The Second 15-Year Housing Plan (1975-1990) aimed at a target of 1.2 million new units or 80,000 dwellings per year. Net additions after demolitions were set at 550,000-600,000 for the plan period. Demolitions, which represented 19 percent of all new construction in the First Plan period, were anticipated to jump to 50 percent in the Second Plan period. In fact, because the heavily subsidized rents charged by the authorities did not cover maintenance, quality progressively deteriorated; and because subsidy incentives were offered for new construction, it became advantageous to demolish the old units rather than fix them. Much of the demolition has been in small towns and rural areas where new units have been constructed on the same plots occupied by the original units.

As indicated in table 4.3, annual plan targets for the Second Plan period were exceeded during the first five years (1976-1980) when they averaged over 90,000 units per year. Over the next five years (1981-1985), housing production declined to around 74,000 units per year and

Table 4.3   DWELLING UNITS BUILT 1960-89 (Average units
built per year, thousands)

Year/ Period	Budapest	Other Towns	Villages	Total	Units per 1,000 Population
1961-65	10.2	18.6	27.7	56.5	5.6
1966-70	11.8	23.5	30.2	66.5	6.5
1971-75	15.5	36.5	35.7	87.7	8.4
1976-80	17.1	40.3	33.1	90.5	8.5
1981-85	14.9	32.0	27.1	74.0	6.9
1986	10.0	33.3	26.2	69.5	6.5
1987	10.3	25.9	21.0	57.2	5.4
1988	8.5	22.4	19.6	50.5	4.8
1989	9.0	23.1	19.4	51.5	n/a

Source: Parry (1989).

has continued to drop over the last five years to levels of
50,000-60,000 units per year.

It is difficult to tell from available data precisely how
roles have been transformed in recent years in the planning for housing, the control and development of land,
and the provision of infrastructure. For many years, the
State Development Agency, the National Savings Bank,
enterprise organizations, local government councils, and
certain forms of cooperative associations had preferential
access to land for multi-unit development. Private individuals could obtain vacant plots to build their own houses
but private contractors were not permitted to assemble
land to build for-sale housing. In 1989 these restrictions

were lifted and an element of competition has been introduced into the system of land and housing development. It appears that a functioning market for land has been established, and households can purchase plots at market determined prices. However, much uncertainty remains about how real estate belonging to state-owned enterprises will be valued and the role local government will take in making serviced plots available for private development.

Beginning in the early 1980s, local governments have experimented in an ad hoc fashion with means of providing plots of land to households for self-help housing. In most cases, households were only able to obtain land if they were employees of a local SOE. The enterprise would intervene on behalf of the employee and negotiate with the local government. The result today is that SOEs are the only organizations experienced in obtaining land for small scale development (compared to the typical large-scale state housing project). However, none of their arrangements have been codified or made routine by local governments. In addition, local SOEs also supported and negotiated on behalf of their employees for small-scale extensions of infrastructure networks to serve their new housing units. It is far from clear that these unplanned interventions are the most efficient method for extending infrastructure networks to serve new development.

Transactions in land and house sales are also marked by inefficiencies. Information on the sale prices is not available from local land registrars. As a result, potential buyers have to undertake the time-consuming task of assembling their own data on recent sales from private sources.

The provision of infrastructure is now apparently under the sole authority of local councils. It is unclear, however, what role the central government continues to play in the allocation of grants to finance capital costs or in the exercise of planning controls. In the past, capital investment was funded from a combination of state development grants, contributions from state-owned, including local council-owned, enterprises. It is also unclear how maintenance is managed and funded. As traditional sources of funds to finance capital and recurrent costs dry up, however, the issue of organizing a new resource base becomes critical.

A reorganization of housing functions at the central government level took place in the summer of 1990, with responsibilities now allocated across five ministries. As of August 1990, it appears that the policy development function is in the Ministry of Social Welfare. Further major shifts are in prospect as the August 1990 law on local governments moves significant responsibilities to the local level. This will become effective after local elections at the end of September.

Construction and Building Materials Industry

Housing construction costs in Hungary have risen dramatically over the last few years, contributing to weak effective current demand. The skyrocketing costs of building materials and the premium prices private builders have to pay for them, as well as the higher cost of second economy labor which produces much of new housing, appear to be the key factors in the rising costs of new housing.

In the period 1987-88 the average construction cost of a new dwelling unit ranged between Ft825,500 and Ft961,700 ($15,575 and $18,145 at the 1988 exchange rate of Ft53 = $1) (Komaromi 1990). This represents a 71 percent nominal increase over 1983 average construction costs, which ranged between Ft516,957 and Ft530,600 ($12,508 and $12,941 at the 1983 exchange rate of Ft41 = $1) (World Bank 1985). In Budapest, average per square meter costs for housing constructed by enterprises and cooperatives (36 percent of all housing units), increased 19 percent from 1987 to 1989. In line with most East European CPEs, housing in Hungary has been produced by state-owned enterprises, cooperatives, and the private sector. As indicated in table 4.4, the construction industry in 1987 employed close to 400,000 workers, or about 8 percent of the total labor force. About 67 percent of these workers were employed in state-owned enterprises or state-supported construction cooperatives. Approximately 32 percent of nongovernmental workers were employed as one- or two-person private contractors.

As documented in table 4.5, there has been a very sharp reduction in the importance of SOEs in housing production in the past several years. By 1988, over 60 percent of all units were privately produced.

State construction enterprises. One of the main elements of Hungary's socialist housing policy was the promotion of state construction enterprises. Designed to meet large-scale production plan targets, they generally employed 4,000 to 6,000 workers, and had monopolistic access to finance, building materials, and serviced land. Despite all the preferential treatment, however, state-sponsored housing still constituted only 40-45 percent of all new construction during 1950-1978 (although in urban areas their share rose to 57 percent).

In recent years, several SOE residential construction firms have ceased operations and more are expected to follow in 1990 and 1991. Some surviving construction SOEs in Hungary are being kept afloat by preferential treatment by the heavily state-owned commercial banks that now manage their accounts, and by virtue of their state status have first access to scarce building materials. It is difficult to say from available data whether some functions are more efficient than others and could be separated

Table 4.4   CONSTRUCTION INDUSTRY ORGANIZATION
AND EMPLOYMENT 1987

Organizational Form	Number of Organi- zations	Workers Employed[a] (thousands)
State constructors	164	190.9
Cooperative constructors	909	74.8
Subtotal	1,073	265.7
Architectural/design and investment enterprises	187	26.5
Specialized industrial and servicing coop groups	403	12.2
In-company economic partnerships	2,305	25.6
Private economic partnerships	2,305	23.7
Small-scale industry[a]	24,917	42.1
Subtotal	30,603	130.1
Total	1,676	395.8

Source: 1988 Hungarian Statistical Yearbook.

a. Licensed craftsmen working as principal occupation or as pensioners.

from parent SOEs and privatized. It is also unclear if the government has any near-term plans for pushing the commercial banks to deny credit to unprofitable construction SOEs. One reason that credit continues to be granted to these enterprises may simply be the absence of skills in the banks to assess credit-worthiness and risk.

Table 4.5   DISTRIBUTION OF NEW HOUSING PRODUCTION
BY TYPE OF BUILDER (percent)

	1976-1980	1981-1985	1986	1987	1988
State building company	46	43	34	37	30
Other organizations	10	7	6	6	5
Private contractors and individuals	44	50	60	57	65
Total	100	100	100	100	100

Source: Ministry of Interior (1989).

The trademark of the SOEs was to build regimented, unattractive, and poor quality housing for a captive market. Interestingly, there are clear signs in Hungary that the remaining SOEs are responding to the declining demand for their housing. With only a minority of their production being purchased for state rental housing, the majority has to be marketed to families--buyers who have become more selective as housing prices and mortgage interest rates have accelerated. In Budapest the better SOEs are introducing much more attractive designs and are building a significant share of their units on a speculative basis. Whether this new found market sensitivity will enable them to survive remains to be seen.

Cooperative sector. One of the most enduring forms of housing development in Hungary is the housing cooperative. Workers in state-owned enterprises, as well as groups of private individuals, form temporary cooperative associations to take advantage of construction subsidies offered to them and preferential access to state-owned lands and building materials. After the construction is completed and the units sold to their members they usually disband. In this model, the actual construction work is done by state-owned enterprises who are contracted for the purpose. More permanent forms of construction coops have been established by larger, multi-purpose or special-purpose cooperatives.[5] Other cooperatives serve housing maintenance functions. In Hungary, as in Poland, housing cooperatives are generally classified, along with construction SOEs, as part of the socialized sector. As access to credit, building materials, and serviced land is equalized in Hungary, cooperatives will have to compete on an equal footing with private contractors in housing and land development.

Private sector. The fundamental distinction in the private sector is between: self-built housing and private contractors and developers building houses for others. Construction businesses on three scales operate in the latter category:

- The day laborer or private tradesman employing only a handful of workers;

- The small-sized firm employing anywhere from 5 to 200 workers;

- The medium-sized company of 200 to 300 employees.

No large private sector construction capacity has emerged, certainly in part because of legal impediments. Although equal access to credit, equipment, and materials is supposedly in place in Hungary, legislation still sets a limit of 500 workers per private company.

According to one source, informal (nonlegalized) sector construction in 1981 constituted about half of private sector residential construction and dominated the maintenance and renovation of privately owned apartments. In the same year 70-80 percent of all maintenance and renovation of private apartments was allegedly carried out in this second economy (Galasi and Sziratzky 1985). If this is true and the share of the second economy in housing construction has been maintained up to the present time, the implications are significant. The much higher wages in the second economy could be driving building costs up; and unrecorded, unpaid taxes on earned income have a direct effect on the revenue stream of government.

There is some evidence that the government is interested in transforming what was previously a top-heavy production structure into a pyramid-shaped one. The pyramid would have a large group of small contractors at the bottom and a proportional number of medium-sized contractors in the middle. Their combined capacity would be sufficient to respond to a range of construction job sizes (World Bank 1989c).

Numerous and serious constraints exist for the small and medium-sized contractor. Some of the more important ones include:

- Restrictions on ability to import required building products and modern, appropriate scale equipment and tools not available in the domestic market;

- Poor access to commercial credit (how much this is a function of the lack of experience in the commercial banking sector in terms of assessing the creditworthiness of real profit-making firms and how much is simply bureaucratic inertia and timid conservatism is unknown);

- Weak contract management skills that impede efficient expansion and ability to participate in bid competition (which is reported to have increased from 3 percent in 1983 to 24 percent of contracts in 1988, an impressive jump);

- Lack of skilled labor, especially in traditional skill areas such as plastering, carpentry, framing, and masonry;

- Undifferentiated and onerous administrative procedures (such as uniform tax reporting forms for the smallest or largest firms).

The majority of private sector production, however, is through self-help which is the dominant type of production outside Budapest. Typically three or four families work in concert to develop their homes together. These tend to be high quality, large units, developed at around half the cost of similar developer-constructed housing (if the value of contributed labor is ignored). Plots are purchased privately and infrastructure services may or may not be provided initially to the plots; the difficulty with obtaining new, serviced plots explains the popularity of demolishing an old structure and building a new one on an already serviced plot. The family-builder usually spends about four years building his unit and engages in a variety of barter and cash transactions to pay for skilled workers to help with key tasks (Hegedus, forthcoming).

Although the self-help approach is being successful in producing a large volume of housing, it is clearly inefficient in that the builders often lack essential skills, capital is tied up for years before it begins to yield housing services, and the builders are often only able to devote time to this task by shorting their regular jobs. Self-help housing is appropriately viewed as a rational response to very high housing price to income ratios and inefficiency in financial and labor markets--financial markets do not provide loans to pay for development (with reasonable structured repayment schedules) and labor markets do not facilitate the builders taking second jobs in the fields in which they are trained.

Building materials industry. There is a paucity of current data describing the structure and general performance of the building materials industry in Hungary. What data exist suggest that the state still continues to hold a dominant--though not monopoly--position on building materials production and distribution. Up until 1985, the industry was organized as described below.

On the production side, the major inputs for residential construction such as cement, lumber, and steel were all produced by SOEs. Private sector competition has been opened up since 1985 for some building materials such as red bricks, insulation, roofing and floor tiles. It is not known whether equal or partial access has been granted to private firms for the manufacture of construction equipment, tools, hardware, and fixtures, for example.

On the distribution side, in 1985 the dominant distribution channels belonged to state entities. Some producers (e.g.,steel, cement) supplied materials directly to the construction SOEs and cooperatives on a priority basis and then filled orders for private firms. Most other building products were distributed through a network of building materials distribution centers (EPTEK) and consignment stores run by EPTEK which sell building materials in smaller quantities (World Bank 1985). As of early 1990 building materials were sold by both state and private stores. Small contractors purchase from private stores, whose prices are only moderately higher than those of the state stores. However, consistency of availability is a problem. More important is the poor quality of many items produced by the SOEs. The constraints facing the industry include:

- Perceived inability of existing light industry to manufacture the range of products, tools, and equipment needed to construct high quality, non-prefabricated residential housing;

- Lack of management skills and technological know-how inhibiting development and growth of productive private building materials producers and distributors;

- Lack of private sector access to commercial credit to finance plant, equipment, and inventories;

- Perceived lack of competition in the building materials distribution system;

- Lack of clarity on the structure and operation of the building materials distribution system.

Housing Allocation and Tenure

Uniform rent controls were introduced in Hungary in 1950. By 1970, rents consumed only about 2-3 percent of the average household budget (utilities were more expensive than rents). Maintenance costs were estimated to be three times as high as the municipal agency received from rents (Baross 1987).

The first Housing Reform of 1971 ushered in a compli-
cated multichannel system of allocating housing and
subsidies. Apartments and applicants were classified by
categories. A queuing mechanism was introduced that
ordered applicants by social status, number of children,
per capita income, socio-political merits, and other non-
welfare measures. Local authorities were in charge of allocating flats to households. The reform also required that
families assigned to them pay a "housing user fee," or "key
money." As explained by Daniel and Partos (1989), the
process proceeded as follows:

> Dwellings built according to different constructions
> schemes received different amounts of state subsi-
> dy, reflected either in the amount of the apart-
> ment's key money in the price of the apartment, or
> in the terms of the loan. The various construction
> schemes were as follows (in order of decreasing
> state subsidy):
>
> - State-owned rental dwellings allocated by local
>   authorities to low-income applicants, where the
>   tenant had to pay key money for the apartment
>   in addition to rent;
>
> - Dwellings sold by the local authorities to appli-
>   cants with the higher per capita income;
>
> - Dwellings built with National Savings Bank
>   investment, but sold by local authorities or by
>   the applicant's employer;
>
> - Dwellings built with the investment of housing
>   cooperatives, but sold by local authorities;

- Dwellings both built with National Savings Bank investments and sold by the Bank;

- Dwellings built with the investments of economic organizations (enterprises) and sold by them;

- Privately owned single family houses.

One effect of the allocation criteria was that it resulted in privileged access by the political elite to the most heavily subsidized and best quality housing. The urban elite was able to exploit the housing allocation channel that would provide them with the best housing solution, irrespective of their income (Baross 1987). It was an inefficient use of the housing stock: it targeted subsidies to the building, not to the need of the household, and levied an unequal financial burden on less well-off households.

The Housing Reform of 1982-1983 substantially reduced this differentiation of allocating preferential loans and subsidies according to settlement categories and types of construction. It also unified the system of subsidies for construction based on private sources and the different types of private construction (condominiums, units built by the National Savings Bank investment, privately owned single family houses) received very similar access to preferential loans. The new unified loans carried terms of a 3 percent interest rate and a 35-year loan period. To protect the National Savings Bank from decapitalization resulting from inflation, the state subsidized the gap between mortgage interest rates and the cost of funds (Daniel and Partos 1989).

However, several other types of behavior indicative of market distortions continued unabated. These included the operation of a dual housing market and a "gray" market.

The 1968 economic reform package sanctioned employment outside the formal state and cooperative enterprise sector and led to a flourishing second economy of largely unregulated, higher wages. Additional wage income combined with the value of small plot vegetable growing on the urban fringes may account for 25 percent or more of total household income (Kessides 1990). In the housing sector this had the effect of stimulating savings and the investment of these additional resources in the private production of housing. While this eased the burden somewhat on government expenditures devoted to housing investment, it also exacerbated existing inequalities and distortions in the sector. Those enjoying two streams of income were able to either enter the privately owned housing market or bid up the key money price of rental housing in the gray market.

Households who rent flats from the state can sell their tenancy rights in the gray market, or under a reprivatization initiative can sell their unit back to government, at a price approximating the value of occupancy rights in the gray market. The funds so generated are used to purchase a dwelling, often with subsidies associated with the loans.[6] In this type of market those with several incomes are able to pay a premium to acquire a state flat or purchase a unit, while households with lower incomes who were in the housing queue are often forced to seek sublets in either publicly or privately owned housing. Sublets did not fall under state rent control policies, and a flourishing market in higher priced, often exploitative, sublets has ensued.

The rental market. Hungary has about 800,000 state-owned rental apartments (about 20 percent of the total housing stock of 4.0 million units); over half of these public rental units are concentrated in Budapest. Although rents were increased about 250 percent in the early 1980s and by another 35 percent in early 1990 (inflation is 20 percent), heavy subsidies continue to make rental housing the most attractive and affordable housing option.[7] Total occupancy costs of state rental units are 5-10 percent of household income. Although recent efforts have been made to target subsidies according to the number of children in the family and a basic housing allowance scheme was implemented in 1990, a coherent welfare policy of allocating subsidies according to need has not yet emerged. To reach market levels, rents would have to be increased 400-500 percent from 1989 levels (Wright 1990).

The subsidy policy continues to sustain several inefficient practices (Hegedus and Tosics 1990):

- Even the highest paid workers still enjoy privileged access to low rents;

- Lifetime occupancy rights and large subsidies, together with the high cost of new housing, have created a kind of freeze on the supply of available apartments on the market, which in turn has had a devastating effect on the ability of workers to exploit demand for labor in other locations;

- Even with the increased rent levels, rents collected cover only about 50 percent of the amount needed to cover maintenance.

This last factor has led to an increasingly dilapidated rental housing stock, currently estimated at up to 200,000 units. In Budapest alone, about 120,000 units require extensive renovation. Deferred maintenance constitutes a continuing financial threat to government and is a major reason that government is actively promoting privatization of state flats. The intention is to pass on the accumulated deferred maintenance costs to the purchaser. However, many of the flats offered in the program to date have been the oldest and smallest in the rental stock and are not in demand.

A principal objective in selling the units was to reap a one-time revenue windfall. This objective was not realized as tenants in deteriorating buildings were reluctant to buy the units and because government provided huge subsidies to the purchasers--in terms of low prices (units sell for as little as 15 percent of value) and 3 percent interest on 15-year installment contracts from OTP. Even with these generous conditions, only about 10 percent of state rental units have been sold to date.

The private ownership market. The average price of a new dwelling unit in 1988 was reported to be Ft2 million--or $37,735 at the 1988 exchange rate (Parry 1989). This is more than twice the reported average cost of construction in 1988. An average housing unit is now estimated to cost 10-14 times the average household income in Hungary.[8] In contrast, this ratio is 2.5 for some developed countries and 5 to 6 for most developing countries. However, the estimate for Hungary does not include all second economy income and therefore may be overstated (Wright 1990). In any event, housing affordability--aggravated by high interest rates as described below--remains one of the most perplexing and pressing issues in the sector today.

One emerging feature in the private housing delivery system is creation of a largely private real estate service industry, which is addressing the needs of the lively market for home purchase. By the middle of 1989, 55 real estate broker companies were reported to have set up shop, 30 of them in Budapest. Commissions average 2-3 percent. Although the shift to the brokerage system from the state setting home sales prices is reported to have caused a 15-20 percent increase in home prices, it has also

widened the range of choices for the home seller who previously had to rely exclusively on OTP and other banks to
price their house (Parry 1989). Each local council also
operates a real estate office to serve buyers and sellers of
the housing stock and the land it owns.

Housing Finance

Finance for housing includes both development or construction period finance and take-out or mortgage financing. The situation in Hungary is somewhat different from
other CPEs due to the government's experimentation with
indirect instruments over the past twenty years.
Development period financing. The story here is very
simple. Commercial banks lend to the large construction
enterprises at standard rates for residential as well as other
development. Such financing is not always needed, however. When the state allocates funds for the production of
housing by SOEs, the funds are made available to finance
the project's development costs. On the other hand, small
builders have very limited access to development period
credit facilities. Beginning in 1989, interest rates on these
loans have been at market rates.

In the same year the central bank offered attractive re-
discounting terms on construction period loans, conditional on rapid project development (under 18 months). This
facility, designed to encourage more lending and lending
to small firms, has been used exclusively by the SOEs and
appears to have failed to meet its primary objective. A
clear impediment to more lending is the lack of underwriting skills at the commercial banks.

Take-out financing. The terms under which long-term
finance was provided prior to 1989 is a complex story, a
complexity which parallels the numerous distinct channels

through which housing was developed and delivered as described earlier. The watershed in housing finance prior to 1989 was the package of reforms implemented in 1983, which imposed a fairly unified set of financing terms on households, regardless of which housing distribution "channel" they were acquiring their unit through. The standard terms were an interest rate of 3 percent on a 35-year loan; maximum loan-to-value ratios were 60 to 70 percent, although these were seldom reached because of loan principal maximums (Daniel and Partos 1989). The state granted a modest up-front subsidy, which varied with family size. If the cost of a unit exceeded a norm, the interest rate was 8 percent, the term reduced to 15 years, and a lower maximum loan-to-value ratio applied; however, apparently only a small number of units fell into this category.[9] The OTP in urban areas, with its 600 branches, and savings cooperatives in the countryside were the only institutions providing mortgage credit.[10]

The 1989 reforms simultaneously moved housing finance toward market conditions and then introduced whole new clusters of subsidies to insulate home purchasers from the impact of higher interest rates on housing affordability. As noted earlier, among the innovations introduced in the reform package were:

- Moving interest rates on new mortgages up substantially, from 3 percent to an effective rate of 18.8 percent (in 1990 rates were raised to 24.5 percent, closer to--but still not at--a market rate); the attempt to raise interest rates on outstanding loans was, however, declared by the courts to be illegal;

- Making the standard loan instrument an adjustable rate mortgage (however, it is still not clear to what index interest rate changes have been tied, what the schedule for adjustments is, and whether there are consumer protections included);

- Permitting direct competition between commercial banks and the National Savings Bank, on both the asset and liability sides of the balance sheet; while some commercial banks have begun competing sharply for deposits from individuals, they are generally approaching consumer lending--including mortgage lending--cautiously.

A very recent and positive step in diversifying and expanding real estate lending has been creation of an independent, private financial institution in Budapest, the Real Estate Bank Ltd. This institution, which is a subsidiary of the Hungarian Credit Bank (MHB), will specialize in financing for commercial and residential development and offer real estate brokerage services (Parry 1989).

The subsidy system introduced at the same time consists of up-front grants or remissions and reductions in the mortgage payments required, i.e., interest payments are reduced.[11] All borrowers with children receive both types of subsidies, although the amount of each subsidy received by a household depends on its size--larger households get larger subsidies. (Childless couples only get the mortgage payment subsidy.) While there is a single program for up-front subsidies (the Socio-Political Subsidy), there are three different interest payment subsidies for which a household can qualify.[12] They are additive. The interest subsidies last for 15 years and are reduced in steps over time. Apparently for childless couples there is a single reduction to a lower level at the end of the fifth year of the mortgage; for families with children there are steps at the end of the fifth and tenth years. Thus, taken as a whole, the system can be fairly complex. The effects of these subsidies can be summarized with reference to two cases.

- A childless couple purchasing a Ft3.4 million home with a 70 percent loan would not receive the downpayment subsidy. They would obtain 30 percent relief on their mortgage payment for the first five years and a 15 percent reduction over the next ten years.

- A family of four purchasing a Ft4.3 million unit with a 70 percent loan would receive a Ft200,000 subsidy for its downpayment. Mortgage interest payments would be reduced by 36.6 percent for the first five years, 33 percent for the next five, and 31 percent for years eleven through fifteen, at which time the subsidies end.[13]

Chiquier (1990) estimates that for a family with two children, for example, the present value of the interest subsidies on a typical loan is equivalent to about 34 percent of the loan principal. Obviously, these subsidies are deep, similar of those granted higher income American households through the tax system. It should be emphasized, however, that beginning in 1989 these subsidies are being explicitly financed from the budget, with OTP being reimbursed for its lost interest charges. Thus in contrast to earlier periods, government knows the cost of these subsidies accurately. Overall, the housing finance system in Hungary has been and continues to be used as a wide channel for directing subsidies to homeowners.

Beyond these subsidies, more help is available for home purchasers. Both employers (SOEs) and local governments provide significant assistance for downpayments (Ft100,000-Ft150,000) to a large share of purchasers. How beneficiaries are selected is not clear.

Overview of Housing Sector Subsidies

There has been frequent mention of the subsidies in the housing sector. This section briefly summarizes the overall situation as of 1989. Aggregate subsidies, fully accounted for, are staggering: about 7.5 percent of GDP. Obviously, reducing and rationalizing these enormous subsidies will be central to any economic reform package.

It is useful to divide existing subsidies between those that are recognized by Government and those that are not.[14] The upper portion of table 4.6 lists the subsidies conventionally recognized by government and their magnitude for 1989 as estimated by the National Planning Organization. The total of Ft82.1 billion represents about 4.9 percent of GDP. Among these, the subsidies closing the gap between the 3 percent mortgage loan rate and the current cost of funds for mortgages originated by OTP between 1983 and the end of 1988 account for half of the total. Overall subsidies to homeowners account for about three-fourths of all subsidies; in other words, homeowners receive subsidies approximately in proportion to their share of all households.[15] Budget outlays by both the national and local governments for state rental housing (the first two items in table 4.5) were about Ft21 billion or 25 percent of the total.

The picture changes modestly when three additional subsidy forms are included in the tabulation, although they are officially "off budget". Employers and local councils together provide about Ft11 billion in assistance to new homeowners. Half of employers' assistance is tax deduct-

Table 4.6   SUBSIDIES TO THE HOUSING SECTOR IN 1989

	Amount (Ft billions)
Recognized Subsidies	
Construction of rental flats	6.4
Maintenance of public rental flats	
-- from state budget	8.6
-- from council subsidies	8.5
Local council subsidy for preparation of building plots, infrastructure	7.0
Socio-political allowances (assistance with downpayments)	10.0
Interest rate subsidies for loans issued before 1989	41.1
Subsidy for early mortgage prepayment	2.0
Interest rate subsidy for loans issued in 1989 or after	1.5
Subtotal	82.1
"Off-Budget" Subsidies	
Homeownership grants from employers	8.0
Homeownership grants from local councils[a]	3.0
Unmeasured rent subsidies	33.0
Subtotal	44.0
Total	126

Source: Buckley et al., (1990), Annex 2.

a. Includes both grants and the principal of low interest rate loans made that year. Data for valuing the interest subsidies on all outstanding loans are not available.

ible, but for enterprises operating at a loss and being supported by public funds, the whole subsidy is effectively a public expenditure.

The largest omission, however, in accounting for housing sector subsidies, is the forgone rental income on the housing stock, i.e., the difference between what the tenant pays and the market rent. Under the widely cited assumption that rent charged on the average state unit is about 20 percent of the market determined rent on the same unit, then the total increment in rents would be about Ft33 billion.

Overall, then, the subsidies to the sector in 1989 were about Ft126 billion, or 7.5 percent of GDP. Of that total, about 42 percent is associated with state rental housing, and the balance goes to homeowners.

Notes, chapter four

1. Thomas 1989: "For example, fiscal balance has been achieved in part by tightening wage and price controls, putting quotas on imports, and increasing taxes on entrepreneurial activity, rather than addressing the "black hole" of governmental and quasi-governmental expenditures."

2. This is based on Thomas (1989).

3. The Center for Privatization, through a grant from A.I.D.'s Private Enterprise Bureau, will be providing both technical assistance and training to the NPA, as well as a long-term advisor (Levintow and Farley 1990).

4. The most important of these were codified in 1989 with the passage of the Act of Foreign Investment, The Companies Act, The Transformation Act. The effect of these Acts is particularly important in several areas (U.S. Department of Commerce 1989):

- A foreigner can own up to 100 percent of a newly-established joint venture company and up to 80 percent equity share in a Hungarian company that has issued shares;

- A joint venture may acquire real property necessary for the conduct of its business (though not speculate in land or establish real estate firms)

- Tax exemptions for up to 5 years are available to firms investing in selected industries with high export earning potential;

- Foreigners can open and maintain hard currency accounts, including, in March 1990, at any commercial bank;

- Joint ventures can repatriate their profits under a limited convertability arrangement for the forint.

5. An example is NOVARAT, a coop of 860 employees that grew out of a larger parent agricultural coop. NOVARAT is engaged in the design and construction of new housing, as well as project management and manufacturing of some building products. They issued bonds to finance construction. These bonds were guaranteed by the state (until government guarantees for bonds were discontinued in 1987). NOVARAT sells single family houses and individual flats (as condominiums) to people with remittances (Elwan 1990).

6. The exact rules governing when a former occupant of a state rental is eligible for homeownership subsidies are quite complex.

7. The rent increase was effectively higher because the tenants were made fully responsible for the cost of internal renovation of their units (formerly half was paid by the government) and significant water and sewerage charges were imposed.

8. Though reliable income data is notoriously difficult to come by in Hungary, one source reports average household income in 1988 at Ft220,000, which (at $1=Ft53) is $4,150 per year or $345 per month (Parry 1989). This includes income from all sources and from all persons in the household. Hence, it is much larger than the average "first economy" monthly wages cited earlier.

9. Data on loan terms from Ministry of Finance (1983).

10. Beyond the subsidized loans from OTP, home purchasers could obtain additional assistance from three sources: interest free loans from employers for Ft100,000 to Ft150,000; a "social allowance for children" which in the 1980s covered about 10 percent of the cost of construction; and, local council grants which only began in 1986 and provided Ft100,000 to Ft150,000 (Daniel and Partos 1989, 18).

11. This description relies heavily on Parry (1989) and Chiquier (1990).

12. The first two are the General and the Dependent subsidies. The third is conditioned to a household having participated in a contract savings scheme.

13. It is not clear whether households can still obtain additional subsidies from their employers, local councils and through the "social allowance for children" which were available prior to 1989.

14. This description relies heavily on Buckley et al. (1990), Annex 2.

15. In early 1990 a new downpayment grant program was created which provides Ft150,000 to young households purchasing a home. It is estimated that this will entail about Ft3 billion in subsidies annually.

Chapter Five

THE HOUSING SECTOR IN POLAND

Among CPEs, Poland has a relatively long history of reform aimed at decentralizing decision-making within the economy. These reforms, beginning in the mid-1950s, produced little real movement away from the CPE paradigm until 1981. In that year, with the economy in crisis, the most complete set of reforms to date was introduced. However, poor economic conditions and resistance by the administrative apparatus of the state to the proposed scaling-back of its powers limited the results of these reforms. In late 1987, a second stage of reform was launched, which freed the economy from central control to a considerable extent but did little to impose discipline on state-owned enterprises.

The inflation and instability that followed has prompted a third round of reform. This stage, the so-called "Big Bang" that went into effect in January 1990, abandons the incremental approach of previous reforms and attempts an economic restructuring that will rapidly transform Poland into a market economy. The reforms are based on a convertible currency, free prices, and operational freedom for state enterprises, while severely cutting back state spending and support and imposing market rates on previously "soft" lending.

These reforms significantly alter the conditions under which state enterprises function and the prices faced by consumers. These changes will be felt particularly strongly in the housing sector, which has been dominated by state producers and functioned with state subsidies (both through capital grants and soft financing).

This chapter examines the course of reforms in the economy that affect the housing sector and changes in the housing sector itself. The first section describes the demographic and economic context to which the housing sector responds. The following sections describe the structure of the sector and how it is changing in response to the reforms.

DEMOGRAPHIC TRENDS

Population growth in Poland has come in cycles caused by population losses and growth slowdowns during the World Wars. Low birth rates, high mortality, and epidemics of typhoid and influenza devastated the Polish population during World War I. The slow growth during 1939-45 was followed by a dramatic baby boom that echoes through succeeding population cohorts (World Bank 1987). The result is a population age structure that is unusually irregular. The current increase in youngest age cohorts is the first echo of the post-war baby boom.

Just as the number of births is affected by the baby boom, so too is the number of elderly persons. Currently, the Polish population is marked by a low proportion of persons over age 65 relative to other industrialized countries. Their numbers will grow slowly for the next 20 years (see table 5.1). Coupled with low levels of fertility,

Table 5.1   POLAND--POPULATION TRENDS 1970-2000

	1970	1980	1990	2000
Total population (millions)	32.7	35.6	38.5	40.8
Percent of total				
Age 14 and under	26.9	24.3	24.9	21.7
Age 15-64	64.8	65.6	65.1	66.3
Age 65 and over	8.3	10.1	10.0	12.0
Dependency ratio[a] (percent)	54.4	52.4	53.6	50.7
Urban population (percent)	52.3	58.2	63.2	66.8
Annual growth (percent)				
Total	0.7	0.9	0.7	0.6
Urban	1.6	1.9	1.4	1.0
Rural	-0.2	-0.5	-0.4	-0.3

Source: United Nations (1986).

a. The dependency ratio is the sum of the population under age 15 and age 65 and over divided by the population aged 15-64 expressed as a percentage.

this will push down the dependency ratio. However, a rapid increase in the number of elderly persons will follow as the age cohort bulge begins to move past age 65. Through higher medical costs and increased pension payments, this will place a heavy burden on the social welfare system.

Over the coming ten years, net population growth in rural areas will continue the negative trend that began in the 1960s. Urban population growth, which peaked in the decade immediately following World War II, remains positive, but is slowing its pace. This deceleration is driven mainly by lower fertility rates and slowed migration from rural areas. The present effect of these demographic changes is high demand for housing, health services, and primary education in urban areas--a situation that will persist for the coming decade. This demand will ebb, but will be followed by another round in approximately 20 to 30 years as the second echo cohort of the baby boom begins to be felt while the original baby boom cohort starts to move into retirement age.

OVERVIEW OF THE ECONOMY[1]

Poland began its reform efforts in 1981 with policy revisions designed to decentralize decision-making, adjust the structure of prices, and make state enterprises more financially responsible. Only slight improvements were achieved from these changes, which were incomplete and not fully implemented by the bureaucracy they sought to control. In addition, the recovery the reforms hoped to promote was limited by slumping world economic conditions, a large foreign debt burden, and domestic imbalances that served as a disincentive to increased labor productivity.

A second round of reform--with aims similar to the first attempt, but also including modifications to relative prices, subsidies, and real wages--was launched in 1987. Conflicts over price and wage adjustments led to rapidly rising real wages and spiralling prices: nominal wages rose 33 percent in 1987 and 63 percent in 1988; open inflation increased from 25 percent in 1987 to 60 percent in 1988

(Government of Poland 1989). Imbalances in the economy worsened rapidly, aggravated by the combination of stagnating output, high levels of demand fueled by rising incomes, excessive monetary expansion to finance a growing budget deficit, and inadequate savings incentives. After five years of economic growth averaging 4 percent annually, the Polish economy contracted by at least 1 percent in 1989 (see table 5.2).

A third reform program, begun in January 1990, is being implemented to achieve two central aims: (1) stabilize the economy quickly by slowing inflation and eliminating shortages; and (2) transform the economic system through greater use of market-based mechanisms. This reform program will consolidate and extend the changes set in motion by the previous two efforts.

The remainder of this section will examine reforms to date and planned changes in three areas:

- State enterprises and the private sector;

- The financial system and fiscal policy;

- Wages and prices.

Reforms in these areas affect the conditions under which housing producers operate, the financing and subsidies available for housing, and the affordability of housing to households.

State Enterprises and the Private Sector

Reforms since 1981 have tried to equalize the conditions under which state and private enterprises operated. Most of these changes--concerning enterprise autonomy, owner-

Table 5.2   ECONOMIC INDICATORS 1986-90 (Percentage change at constant prices)

	1986	1987	1988	1989[b]	1990[c]
GDP	4.2	2.0	4.12	-1.0	-5.0
Retail prices	18	25	60	252	395
Real wages	3	-3	15	7	-31
Budget deficit (percent of GDP)	1.1	3.5	1.4	8.1	0.8
Current account[a] ($ million)		-417	-580	-2,029	-3,033

Source: IMF (1990).

a. Trade in convertible currencies only.
b. Estimated.
c. Projected.

ship, and financial responsibility--were focused on the state sector. But some lifted restrictions on private firms and attempted to increase competition in the economy.[2]

In 1981, "first stage" enterprise reforms allowed:

- Most state enterprises to set their own production targets and to control investment, sources of input supply, and level of employment;

- Workers' self-management through an elected workers' council at each enterprise;

- Possible liquidation for enterprises demonstrating continued unprofitability;

- Increased competition through freedom for state enterprises to expand production into new areas and loosened restrictions on private small-scale activities.

In practice, supervising ministries and planning agencies still controlled enterprises both directly (through programs for key commodities or noncompetitive government procurements) and indirectly (through command over access to inputs and foreign exchange). In 1986, government controlled the production of over 100 items and the allocation of half the material inputs in the economy.

Workers' councils started functioning in 1983, but never became influential in enterprise management. Personnel and management decisions continued to be dominated by ministerial authorities.

The law on bankruptcy, passed in 1983, provided for a lengthy process before an enterprise could be liquidated. Most enterprises facing difficulty were able to avoid being classed as bankrupt through negotiations with government that provided subsidies or preferential allocation of inputs. The few liquidations that did take place were typically mergers or restructuring rather than a declaration of bankruptcy and sale of assets to pay creditors.

The reforms did not increase competition. State enterprises were uninterested in expansion during a time of economic difficulty and while remaining subject to government control. Regulations that imposed additional restrictions and taxes on the sector later hindered the expansion of small-scale private firms which began with the 1981 reforms.

Beginning in 1987, a second set of reforms again stressed enterprise autonomy:

- Central planners abandoned detailed, substantive targets and the planning and control apparatus was cut back;

- Local authorities assumed responsibility for supervision of most state enterprises;

- Government allowed enterprises to control part of their capital base and to transform themselves into joint stock companies;

- State enterprises faced accelerated bankruptcy proceedings;

- Antimonopoly measures broke up state enterprises to encourage competition within sectors;

- Government imposed uniform tax treatment for both socialized and private enterprises;

- Private enterprises no longer required permission to operate, had no size limits, and were granted equal rights to credit and inputs.

The reforms did have some effect through 1989. The role of central planners and the scope of central control declined. Profitability became a more common benchmark of enterprise performance and bankruptcy proceedings were initiated against 140 enterprises. However, financial discipline remained elusive as ministries still bargained with central government for concessions to support their enterprises.

More decision-making devolved to enterprises and their workers' councils; state ownership became more passive. Little progress was achieved, however, on the creation of joint stock companies or sale of state enterprise property. The effect of these reforms on the degree of concentration and competition was disappointing, however. Some changes took place--the share of recorded private activity in nonagricultural output rose to over 10 percent in 1987 and continued to increase through 1989; almost 300 enterprises were split up in 1988 under antimonopoly regulations. But their effects were small against the remaining bulk of the socialized economy.

The 1990 reform program is intended to maintain the momentum behind these earlier reforms (see Government of Poland 1989). Government plans for state enterprises and the private sector include measures to:

- Devise a framework for divesting state ownership, begin the sale of state assets, and establish a securities exchange;[3]

- Break up remaining monopolies, institute antimonopoly regulations, and remove remaining restrictions on setting up new enterprises;

- Eliminate residual elements of central planning and priority for government orders;

- Update the labor code to allow work force adjustments with greater ease;

- Allow creditors to initiate bankruptcies with streamlined procedures;

- Prepare for comprehensive reform in 1991-92 of the budget and tax system (based on a comprehensive income tax and value-added tax).

Financial System and Fiscal Policy

Reform since 1981 attempted to move the financial system away from the passive accommodation of state budget and investment requirements by the banking system to multiple sources of financing that reflect the true cost of capital. On the fiscal side, modifications to the system of taxes and subsidies (through more uniform application of taxes and a simpler tax structure) aimed to impose financial discipline on state enterprises and to achieve equality of tax treatment for state and private enterprises.

Starting in 1981, the first round of reform set out the following changes:

- The Ministry of Finance ceased to have jurisdiction over the National Bank of Poland (NBP), though the NBP still had to coordinate credit availability with the central annual plan;

- Legislation directed state banks only to loan funds to enterprises that met self-financing criteria;

- State banks were allowed to raise interest rates and accept time deposits;

- Government imposed an income (profits) tax on enterprises.

Though the NBP was formally freed from government control, a Banking Council and informal pressures kept it closely linked to ministries and the planning apparatus. Similarly, the government granted waivers and preferential access to credit for a number of activities and sectors. The flow of credit to the state sector, both for investment and working capital, remained substantially unchanged.

Interest rates were raised only marginally and were still negative in real terms. Households had little incentive to save and reduced their excess money holdings through purchases in the second economy. Enterprises with excess cash invested it in expansion projects or stockbuilding. Without positive real interest rates, the financial system failed to actively intermediate between potential savers and borrowers.

The budget deficit fell to an average of less than 1 percent of GDP in 1983-86, due mainly to the elimination of many nonsystematic subsidies. However, the tax system remained a complex set of highly differentiated taxes. Over 400 different turnover tax rates, ranging from 0 to 90 percent, applied to sales of different products. In addition, enterprises sought relief from the income tax and other taxes to replace the subsidies that had been eliminated. This created a wide range of effective tax rates among sectors and enterprises.

The second stage of reform (starting in 1987) recognized the importance of resolving issues which the 1981 reforms did not tackle: establishing positive real interest rates; making the banking system more independent and a better financial intermediary; and simplifying the tax system. The government took the following steps:

- Nominal interest rates were raised;

- A two-tier banking system was established with commercial banks, independent from the NBP, operating on a self-financing basis without restraints;

- Bonds could be issued by any legal entity and purchased by both enterprises and individuals.

However, the functioning of the credit market showed little improvement. The accelerating inflation of 1987-89 wiped out the effects of higher nominal interest rates, keeping them negative in real terms. The growth of credit was more expansionary that planned. The central government budget deficit grew under inflationary pressures that drove up expenditures on subsidies (particularly for food, housing, and energy) and eroded the real value of periodic tax payments.

The new institutional structure of the credit market did indicate a strong desire to press ahead with reform. The new independent banks--the former state banks (such as PKO Savings Bank) and nine new regional commercial banks--were, in principle, freed to compete in the provision of all banking services to all customers. Bond issues were actively encouraged by the removal of restrictions on their use. It is still too early to judge the effects of these changes.

The 1990 reform program relies heavily on positive real interest rates as a key economic stabilization and restructuring tool (Government of Poland 1989). Positive real interest rates are necessary to stimulate financial savings, improve the efficiency of investment, and discourage switching into foreign exchange. Fiscal reform, untouched in the second stage, is also an element in the government's current plans. Specific measures include:

- Maintaining positive real interest rates through monthly adjustments to the NBP refinance rate;

- Ending all lending at preferential interest rates and only subsidizing (explicitly from the state budget) lending for agriculture and housing;

- Loosening of reserve requirements and payment of interest on all deposits held within the banking system;

- Establishing the full independence of the NBP with a mandate for maintaining a stable currency;

- Reducing the central budget deficit from 7 percent of GDP in 1989 to 1 percent in 1990 through elimination of most subsidies (except for transport and housing);

- Placing limits on government borrowing and refraining from using the NBP to finance expenditure;

- Planning for a major tax reform in 1991-92 to simplify the tax system using comprehensive corporate and personal income taxes and a value-added tax.

Prices and Wages

Through 1989, changes affecting prices and wages were only slowly and incrementally put into effect. The government remained committed to administered price revisions.

The exchange rate experienced a similar transformation, with slow adjustments gradually moving domestic and border prices together. In all, the trend was toward greater price freedom in the economy.

On the wage side, reforms intended both to promote wage variations that reflected productivity differentials and to restrain the overall growth of enterprise wage bills. The inflationary spiral of 1989-88 is testimony to the failure of these reforms.

In 1981-86, during the first stage of reform, the government took six major steps to reform the system of prices and wages:

- Prices were grouped into three categories:
  -- Administrative prices, set by government, for basic household and production goods,
  -- Regulated prices, set by producers and monitored by government, and
  -- Contract prices, set freely in the market place;

- Controlled prices were raised;

- Exchange rates for foreign trade were consolidated and simplified along with depreciation (by more than one half) of the zloty in 1982;

- Exporters gained limited access to their foreign exchange earnings and an auction for other enterprises was started;

- Wage rates, within mandated minimum and maximum limits, were freed;

- A series of taxes were imposed on wage bill increases above specified norms.

The changes to the pricing system did reduce imbalances, but not enough to bring markets into equilibrium. The rises in controlled prices were insufficient to offset continued excess demand. While the scope of contract pricing increased during the first reform, producers faced a number of restrictions on price rises, such as limits on price changes and taxes on "excessive" price increases. The reform of the exchange rate failed to translate into an incentive for export within the economy, as the system of price equalization (using taxes and subsidies to bring foreign prices in line with domestic prices) remained in effect.

Enterprises failed to take advantage of their freedom to set wages to reflect productivity. Rather, wages were increased by moving employees up through the wage scale with little regard to qualifications. Other actions by enterprises, such as hiring low-skilled workers to reduce the growth rate of average wages or negotiating exemptions from wage taxes, reduced the effectiveness of taxes in curbing the growth of wage costs.

The government, responding to the deteriorating economic situation, carried on the second stage of reform in 1987-89 with similar approaches to changing the system of prices and wages:

- Goods with regulated prices were shifted to the contract pricing category and the process by which goods were removed from the administered price list was simplified;

- Exporters' returns became more closely linked to world prices and their access to foreign exchange was improved;

- Additional taxes and penalties for excessive wage growth were imposed on enterprises.

The cost of correcting the structure of relative prices, through greater price freedom and bringing domestic prices in line with world prices, was accelerating inflation as wages kept up with--and even exceeded--changing prices. Wages grew despite tax disincentives as enterprises were successful in negotiating exemptions.

To break inflation, the government's 1990 reform program has used the exchange rate and wages to anchor prices once the one-off changes in the price system have worked through the economy (Government of Poland 1989). The major components of the program include:

- Freeing all but a tenth of all prices from administrative control;

- Unifying the exchange rate and defending convertibility after a devaluation of over 10 percent (compared to the December 1989 free market rate);

- Limiting wage increases to only a portion of price rises--enterprises granting higher rises in wages will be liable for taxes (without exemption) at punitive rates.

The program has reduced inflation decisively in 1990, with the monthly rate falling from 80 percent in January to under 5 percent in May. Punitive taxes on wage increases more than 20 percent in excess of inflation have effectively restrained wage increases--but at the cost of reduced output and employment. Officially, output was down by over 30 percent in June compared to the previous year (although this does not take into account the growth of small-scale, private production, which escapes the statistical net).

Unemployment has surged, from virtually nil to 511,000 (3.8 percent of the work force) at the end of June 1990.

THE HOUSING SECTOR[4]

The housing sector in Poland, characterized by the shortages and heavy subsidies found elsewhere in CPEs, has been further weakened by the economic problems since 1981. The disappointing performance of the housing sector reflects the past difficulties in achieving effective reform throughout the economy. Moreover, it indicates a failure to recognize the large costs that a poorly functioning housing system imposes on the economy in terms of subsidy costs, uneven distribution of benefits, inefficient production, and reduced labor mobility.

Housing Stock and Production

Poland exhibits the most severe housing shortages in Eastern Europe. Although other countries have succeeded in overcoming the deficits caused by war-time damage to the housing stock, Poland still has not caught up with its initial post-war shortfall of 1.5 million units. In 1985, the country had 18 percent (or 1.4 million) more households than dwellings.

This deficit manifests itself through lengthy waiting times for housing: over 15 years in major cities; over 5 years in smaller cities. Turnover in the housing stock has virtually stopped as households seek to retain whatever housing they have been able to obtain.

Poland's persistent housing deficit is explained mainly by its low levels of investment and productivity in the sector (compared to countries with similar incomes or housing deficits)--see table 3.1 in chapter 3. The share of housing in total investment declined from 16 percent in 1965 to 13 percent ten years later. Since the mid-1970s, in response to improved economic conditions and public pressure, the share of housing in total investment has risen to over 20 percent (Matras 1989a). However, lagging productivity in the sector and rising unit costs have prevented these gains in resources from translating into higher real output. In fact, the per capita number of dwellings completed, after rising initially, has fallen to 4.1 units per 1,000 persons in 1989 from its 1979 peak of 8.1 units per 1,000 persons.

Like other CPEs, in the post-war era there were three main sources of new housing in Poland: the state, cooperatives, and private firms. Following World War II, the state stepped up its role and provided an increasing share of new housing. In the late 1950s, the state had begun to shift its resources to housing developed by cooperatives; by 1965, they were the major source of new housing. About half the current housing stock is privately owned; the rest is about evenly split between state-owned and cooperative housing.

The different stages of economic reforms have caused the control of housing development, production of dwellings, and allocation of units to change over the past decade; further change is certain under the current reform program. These steps in the housing production process are examined in turn below.

Planning, Land, and Infrastructure

The public sector still retains a dominant position in developing land for housing. The majority of urban land in Poland is owned by the state; only 30 percent is privately owned (World Bank 1990). Reform has, in principle, made these state lands available for sale and development. However, pending an inventory (now under way) and clarification of ownership of urban land, no state-owned land can be transferred.

Land use planning in cities has usually focused on zoning and reserving large parcels of land suitable for development with blocks of apartments using industrialized, prefabricated panel techniques. These sites, often on the periphery of cities, traded easy access to the builders with expensive infrastructure extensions to the site. This pattern is being maintained in Warsaw; the municipal planning office is proposing to concentrate future housing production on three very large sites (World Bank 1990).

Land use plans often specify low-density development (particularly in those areas designated for single-family housing) to counter environmental problems caused by inadequate infrastructure. (Cities are responsible for infrastructure planning, but in the past had to rely on centralized agencies for implementation.) As a result, urban housing is often developed without access to piped sewerage and lacking connections to gas and heating networks. Thus, residential sites are overly large (to safely accommodate septic tanks) and coal is used for home heating (contributing to air pollution). This pattern of development, requiring excessive investment to extend trunk infrastructure, contributes to inefficient consumption of land and increasing urban sprawl.

Shortages of infrastructure and inefficient use of urban land exert a strong influence on the price of land sold in the "free" market for housing. The price of agricultural land on the periphery of large urban areas increases by 200 to 400 percent when it becomes available (without services) for residential development. Fully serviced land can raise the price another tenfold. This price for serviced land is two to three times the cost of providing infrastructure.

Though there are no formal restrictions on land sales (apart from the current freeze on transfers pending the land inventory), individuals and private construction firms have several obstacles to overcome to obtain land and permission to build. For example, development rights are granted to the applicant and not tied to the land parcel; sale of the developed land or housing unit requires the purchaser to repeat parts of the approval process. Gaining development permission also involves obtaining similar approvals from different levels of the administrative system. Recent changes to the Spatial Planning Act guarantee equal access for all types of investors (state, cooperative, or private), but land use planning and development approvals remain complex.

Prior to reform, when large subsidies were available for housing, the real cost of providing developed land was not reflected in the price charged. Direct subsidies for land development and infrastructure are still available through the Land Management Fund (financed by a 1.5 percent tax on construction) and the Housing Economy Fund (World Bank 1990). Despite changes through the Land Use and Expropriation Act of 1985, which mandated a commercial basis for the sale of state-owned land, state bureaucracies still make free or underpriced transfers of land to housing investors. This has caused land hoarding, particularly by cooperatives who receive land but lack the resources for land development and construction. With uncontrolled pricing and elimination of subsidies, land and infrastructure standards will have to be tailored to meet a market test of affordability rather than simply respond to city planners' view of household needs.

One way to counter some of these problems have already been found by city planners in Krakow. A land use inventory there identified several hundred sites suitable for in-fill housing development. Raising residential densities takes advantage of existing infrastructure networks and obviates the need for costly expansion, on the assumption that the existing infrastructure can handle the increased loads.

Government responsibilities for planning for new housing development have been transferred to local governments. These governments, now led by newly elected officials, are deciding how to proceed, including assessing how to finance infrastructure investment. As of August 1990, the emerging patterns are unclear.

Construction and Building Materials Industry

Housing production in Poland exceeded 250,000 units annually during the latter half of the 1970s. In the 1980-88 period annual production slowed to 193,000 units as economic conditions deteriorated. Production in 1989 is estimated at only 149,000 units (World Bank 1990), the lowest level since the 1960s. Some of this decline can be traced to the problems of the construction sector.

Producers of housing in Poland are divided into two main groups:

- Large, state-owned building enterprises (*kombinats*) mainly building apartments (about 140,000 units in 1988) for cooperatives or for state-owned rental housing;

- Small-scale private builders mainly building single-family houses in rural areas and small cities (about 50,000 units in 1988).

Kombinats. The kombinats are the largest producers in the sector, but have traditionally been more concerned with production volume than meeting household needs. They are vertically integrated and control many of the producers of building materials for the construction industry. Kombinats rely on prefabrication technology that uses large-scale panels for constructing multistorey apartment blocks. The process is capital- and energy-intensive and the production plant and equipment represent high fixed costs for the producers; labor accounts for only 15 percent of the cost of the panels (World Bank 1990). The factories are large and designed to operate at high volumes of production. As a result, the kombinats dominate their local area in a monopolistic fashion.

Under central planning, the kombinats provided housing units in response to requests channelled through the planning agencies (who also controlled funding for land development and infrastructure provision). The large capital costs of their technology could only be covered by developing large sites with thousands of similar units. To meet their goal of keeping housing production volume up, the planners had to develop housing in suburban and peripheral urban areas to respond to the technological and cost structures of the kombinats. This approach led to low average residential densities in cities and pushed up infrastructure costs.

Reliance on this construction technology, intended to meet chronic housing shortages through high-volume production, demonstrates several weaknesses:

- The design of units is rigid and monotonous and does not offer the choice households are beginning to demand;

- Variations in panel dimensions and damage in transit lead to frequent onsite repairs, poor joints and assembly, high maintenance costs;

- The technology is not labor-saving as planned because of the extensive field work required to correct factory flaws and transport damage.

The results of these problems are housing units that, in terms of both household satisfaction and cost, compare unfavorably with traditional housing construction.

Productivity in state construction, after rising during the 1970s, has fallen in the 1980s. At present about 160,000 units remain unfinished (World Bank 1990). The average time required to complete a state housing project increased from 17 months in the 1970s to 27 months in the 1980s. Housing unit costs have risen steeply. There are a variety of causes for this poor performance:

- Kombinats often operate far below their theoretical capacity during economic slowdowns and pass on their high fixed costs into the cost of their housing;

- Labor productivity has fallen as kombinats have failed to reform their wage policies or restructure their workforce;

- There are shortages of building materials, fittings, and tools and equipment and lack of coordination with infrastructure installation is lacking.

Private builders. The private sector construction industry has grown despite being hampered by the dominant role of the kombinats. Most private builders employ only a few workers--until 1988, a private company could not have more than six employees--and have faced difficulty trying to expand. The kombinats, employing thousands, control most construction workers. The industrial approach to house-building has reduced the numbers of conventional building tradesmen and as well as supplies of traditional building materials. Private construction firms have also been constrained by their lack of access to building materials, credit, and construction equipment. In spite of these problems, activity by private builders was expanding (until the recent price surges caused by price deregulation) in response to the removal of restrictions on private firms.

Productivity in the private sector is also low; over 100,000 units remain unfinished in urban areas. The average construction period for private housing units is six years (World Bank 1990). Apart from materials shortages and financing difficulties, the pace of private housing construction is often slowed because of administrative restrictions. One of the principal factors in the long construction period is the regulation, lifted in January 1990, forbidding a household from owning more than one dwelling. As a result of this law, parents would begin construction of a house but delay its completion until one of their children marries and is eligible to occupy one of the units. This rule explains why Warsaw had 15,400 unfinished housing units and only 630 dwellings completed in 1989 (World Bank 1990).

The 1990 reforms should cause major restructuring in the construction industry. Kombinats, which have long received low-cost loans to finance their operations (as well as tax exemptions and production subsidies), will be required to borrow at commercial rates to finance their operations--making units produced at the current two-year pace unsalable to most households. As many as 70 percent of the kombinats have severe financial problems and could face closure in the future. Some enterprises have laid off workers; others may break up into smaller production units and shift production from large panels to smaller components such as window units or precast concrete elements that can be used more flexibly by different builders.

The reforms, which augur poorly for the kombinats, represent an opportunity for the growing private construction industry:

- Construction labor will become available as state construction enterprises close and surplus equipment may be available for lease or purchase;

- The break-up of kombinats into smaller production units could increase and diversify the supply of building components;

- Greater freedom for other private businesses should spur demand for small- and medium-scale construction to build and renovate offices, storefronts, and other workspaces.

In early 1990, local planners gave diverse views of expected construction in the years ahead. Planners in Krakow foresaw the predominance of traditional technology and small builders, while planners in Warsaw foresaw the opposite (World Bank 1990).

An important issue for small construction firms will be access to commercial credit. This capital will allow investments in tools and equipment to expand and increase productivity and be used as construction period financing. It is unclear, however, whether the commercial banks established by the financial sector reforms will be willing or able to undertake this kind of lending. The Ministry of Construction is considering establishing a National Housing Development Bank which could act as a lender to private construction firms.

Housing Allocation and Tenure

As in other CPEs, housing in Poland is obtainable from three sources:

- The state, through state-owned enterprises and local governments;

- Cooperatives, which are now the principle source of new housing units;

- Private housing, almost exclusively single-family dwellings.

Shares of housing investment since 1970 by these three types of investors are shown in table 5.3.

State rental housing. The two types of state housing accounted for 40,000 new units in 1989 (33,000 from state enterprises and 7,000 from local governments), just under a quarter of the new units available (World Bank 1990). These units are built exclusively as rental housing, although some local governments and enterprises have begun selling units to their tenants. In fact, as many as 1.5 million units may have been sold in the last quarter of 1989 as tenants acted in the face of higher interest rates, and rents and utility charges that reflected true costs (see the section on Poland's housing finance below). The government, as yet, has not established a long-term policy on selling off the housing stock or on how to price the units. At present, units are being sold to their occupants at an administratively set price averaging about $1,500, or about 10 percent of their "free" market price.

Enterprises are free to set their own eligibility requirements for access to housing. They also receive indirect subsidies from the state to support construction of this

Table 5.3   INVESTORS IN POLISH HOUSING 1970-85
(percent of total production)

	1970	1975	1980	1985
State and enterprises	23.5	33.5	18.6	22.4
Cooperatives	48.9	43.2	55.7	47.7
Private sector	27.6	23.7	25.7	29.9
Total	100.0	100.0	100.0	100.0

Source: Matras (1989a), United Nations (1988).

housing: financing for half the capital cost (formerly at low rates, but at commercial rates as of January 1990), and exemption from taxation of retained earnings used for housing. Local government housing is available to low-income residents and is also used to attract skilled workers in short supply to the area. Capital costs for this housing are covered through budgetary grants to the local government.

Cooperatives. Cooperatives are the largest source of housing in Poland, providing about half the new units in 1989--73,000 for rental and 12,000 for purchase (World Bank 1990). These units are usually constructed by state construction enterprises.

Cooperatives provide three kinds of tenure for their participants: tenancy, condominium ownership, and ownership of single-family dwellings. In the first two cases, the cooperatives continue to exist after construction of the units is completed. Tenants make "key money" payments equal to 10 percent of the cost of the unit (Frenzen 1990). Members of owner cooperatives have the right to sell their units on the open market. Capital subsidies received from the state must be repaid when the unit is sold (although there are no data on how strongly this regulation is enforced). Tenancy cooperatives do not allow units (or their leaseholds) to be sold. However, tenants can buy out the equity in their unit and gain ownership.

Cooperatives are eligible for "credit remissions" (i.e., government reimbursement of part of the loan to finance construction). These subsidies typically account for 14 percent of total costs for ownership cooperatives and 21 percent for rental cooperatives, assuming typical 70 percent loan-to-value ratios (World Bank 1990). In addition, until January 1990 coop owners were eligible for very low rate loans from the state savings bank (see further below).

Private housing. Private housing is mostly built in small cities and rural areas where state housing is often not available and land is more readily obtainable. Private housing accounted for 39,000 new units in 1989 (World Bank 1990). Private housing units are generally much larger than housing in the socialized sector (in 1984, 101 square meters per unit versus 54 square meters per unit, respectively) and offer greater choice than is available from state or cooperative housing, which relies on industrially produced units. Households that purchase private units also receive credit remissions, intended to boost private housing production, equal to 30 percent of the loan on the house--about 15 percent of total costs in the typical case, with a loan-to-value ratio of 50 percent (World Bank 1990).

There are no restrictions on the sale of private units. The transfer tax on housing sales has been substantially reduced in past years; there is no tax on the purchase of a newly built unit and a 2 percent tax on the sale of an existing unit.

Households that opted for private housing or buying a unit on the free market in the past faced high prices-- caused by inefficient housing production and the shortage of units--relative to their incomes. In 1985, the typical price for a 50 square meter flat was 8 annual incomes at cost and between 12 and 24 annual incomes on the open market. Thus, households could not realistically finance the purchase of housing on their incomes and had to rely on accumulated assets, either through incremental construction or long waits to build up their own financial resources.

The current situation is similarly marked by high prices--now driven by high building materials prices, a result of shortages and price deregulation under the economic reform program--relative to income. Construction costs have now risen to the levels of free market prices in the past; the price of a 50 square meter flat on the private market (at cost) is now 22 annual average incomes (World Bank 1990). These prices are unaffordable to almost any household that requires financing for its house purchase. However, if the current reform program achieves its stabilization objectives, affordability in the housing sector should increase sharply by the end of 1990. Housing prices should fall, mainly due to a decrease in building materials' prices from their peak in early 1990, and the decline of interest rates with falling inflation, reducing the financing cost.

Housing Finance System

In 1990 the dominant issues in the Polish housing finance system are subsidies and affordability in an inflationary environment. Subsidies make up a large part of the government budget deficit, accounting for more than 7 percent of expenditure in 1989, and add to inflationary pressure. As shown in table 5.4, while some subsidies, such as the credit remissions for cooperative and state housing, have fallen in real terms and as a percent of all subsidies in the sector (because of inflation and declining output), other subsidies, such as operating supports for state rental housing, have increased (because of failure to match rent increases with escalating maintenance costs). Until January 1990, when interest rates were raised to market levels, off-budget subsidies granted through below-market interest rates on housing lending increased dramatically with rising inflation in 1988-89.

As noted in the previous section, rapidly rising prices have pushed housing costs outside the affordable range for most Polish households. At the same time, those fortunate enough to occupy state housing spend only about 2 percent of their income on housing and a similar proportion on centrally provided services such as central heating and hot water. Indeed, these "maintenance subsidies" accounted for over half of all sectoral subsidies in 1989 and are expected to top 60 percent in 1990 (see table 5.4).

Until the January 1990 interest rate reform cooperative housing units were typically priced to cost their owners between 5 percent and 12 percent of their monthly income. By comparison, households in other countries with income levels similar to Poland typically spend between 20 percent and 30 percent of their income on housing.

The issues of subsidies and affordability/expenditure apply to both housing purchase--how to eliminate subsidies (or at least make them more effective) while keeping housing affordable--and the operation of the state rental stock--how to raise the proportion of income spent on housing services and make the system self-financing. This section looks at the two areas in turn.

FINANCE FOR HOME PURCHASE

Financing for the purchase of a house or cooperative unit is presently available from only two sources:

- PKO Savings Bank, which is the sole source of mortgage lending for individuals;

- Narodowy Bank Polski, which lends to cooperatives constructing housing.

In principle, the reform of the financial sector allows other banks to undertake lending for housing, but this has not yet happened.

Until January 1990, financing for housing was available to any borrower through fixed-rate mortgages at concessionary rates (World Bank 1990):

- Cooperative tenants (i.e., households that are members of a cooperative and rent units, mainly in apartment blocks, from the cooperative) were eligible for 40-year loans (made to the cooperative) at 3 percent to finance up to 90 percent of the cost of the unit;

- Cooperative owners (i.e., households that are members of a cooperative and purchase their unit, mainly single-family dwellings, from the cooperative) received 40-year loans at 6 percent to finance up to 80 percent of the cost of the unit;

Table 5.4　　POLAND: BUDGET SUBSIDIES TO HOUSING

		1988	
Types of Budgeted Subsidies	Amount	Share of Subsidies (percent)	Share of Budget (percent)
Investment			
Interest rates subsidies on the outstanding portforlio	68.0	9.34	0.67
Remission of credits for cooperative tenants	175.5	24.09	1.74
Utilities and infrastructure (Land Development Fund, Housing Economy Fund, and other local subsidies)	122.4	16.80	1.21
Premium on deposits in State Savings Bank	25.4	3.49	0.25
Total budgeted investment subsidies	391.3	53.72	3.88
Maintenance			
Maintenance and repairs -- to cooperatives -- to state-owned housing	5 151.5	0.69 20.89	
Total	156.5	21.49	1.55
Central heating and hot water -- to cooperatives -- to state-owned housing	147.9 32.7	20.30 4.49	1.47 0.32
Total	180.6	24.79	1.79
Total maintenance subsidies	337.1	46.28	3.34
Total budget subsidies	728.4	100.00	7.22

(billions of Zlotys)

	1989			Projected 1990		
Amount	Share of Subsidies (percent)	Share of Budget (percent)	Amount	Share of Subsidies (percent)	Share of Budget (percent)
455.0	22.63	1.50	2,420.0	17.98	1.25
199.7	9.93	0.66	492.1	3.66	0.25
217.0	10.79	0.72	2,171.0	16.13	1.12
62.0	3.08	0.20	100.0	0.74	0.05
933.7	46.44	3.09	5,183.1	38.52	2.69
8.5	0.42		40.0	0.30	
523.9	26.06		4,633.8	34.44	
532.4	26.48	1.76	4,673.8	34.73	2.42
476.5	23.70	1.57	3092.0	22.98	1.60
67.8	3.37	0.22	507.2	3.77	0.26
544.3	27.07	1.80	3,599.2	26.75	1.86
1,076.7	53.56	3.56	8273.0	61.48	4.29
2,010.4	100.0	6.64	13,456.1	100.00	6.98

Source: World Bank (1990).

- Private owners received 40-year loans at 6 percent subject to limits on the size of the unit (less than 95 square meters) and the loan amount (normally about half the cost of the unit).

With the inflation of the past two years, the interest rates on these loans were highly negative in real terms and granted an indirect subsidy to mortgage holders. This subsidy was regressive since the windfall to the borrower increases with the size of the loan. This indirect subsidy represented 1.5 percent of the national budget in 1989 (World Bank 1990).

The reforms of January 1990 raised interest rates on all new and outstanding lending. Henceforth, the interest rate is to be variable and determined each month by the central bank. The refinancing rate for the PKO Savings Bank for January was set at 34 percent per month, 6 percentage points below the 40 percent rate offered for other lending (table 5.4). Despite the modestly preferential rate, the cost of servicing mortgages under new terms (essentially adjustable rate mortgages with revisions on a monthly basis) has increased explosively. Most households are unable to meet this jump in housing costs; World Bank (1990) calculations show that, in the early months of the 1990 reform, middle-income households will face estimated monthly mortgage payments in excess of 50 percent of monthly income. The increase in payments is being spread out as follows (Government of Poland 1989):

- The borrowing household pays 8 percent of the increase in the mortgage payment;

- The state pays 32 percent of the increase as a subsidy;

- The remainder of the increase in the payment is capitalized into the outstanding debt (which ratchets up the household's payment and the state subsidy).

By the summer of 1990 the rate of inflation had declined sharply and the worst of the "payment shock" was past, at least in this episode of inflation. In principle, raising interest rates and restructuring lending toward adjustable rate mortgages, in conjunction with the other economic reforms, helps lessen some of the worst problems of the housing subsidy system:

- Subsidies are now more "transparent" and can be more effectively targeted on households that need assistance;

- Distortions caused by low-cost finance, such as households waiting years to get a state-sponsored or cooperative unit, are diminished and the private sector is more competitive with the socialized housing producers;

- Households have greater incentive to save for housing because returns are higher on savings and price is becoming a more important factor in the allocation of housing.

It is worth noting, however, that many households with outstanding mortgages may default on loans as the payments increase, if there is a new round of inflation. Under such potentially unstable economic conditions the Dual Index Mortgage may well be more appropriate (see chapter 10).

FINANCING OPERATION OF
THE RENTAL STOCK

As noted above, rents charged to tenants in state-owned rental units are low. At the beginning of 1990, after increases of about 500 percent, which brought rents back to their real levels in 1986, rents still only covered one-fifth of the maintenance costs associated with state rental housing; subsidies for the other four-fifths accounted for 2 percent of the national budget (Frenzen 1990). The share of maintenance in total government subsidies has been increasing in the past two years as materials for repairs have become scarce and more expensive under price deregulation. (Cooperatives, being self-financing, pass almost all the costs of maintenance on to their tenants.)

The subsidy is regressive. It is granted to every tenant, regardless of income, and occupants of larger units receive a proportionately larger benefit.

Part of the reform of 1990 made cost recovery of operations and maintenance a high priority; state owners and managers of rental housing are to be required to collect adequate rents to cover their costs. This implies an average fivefold increase in rents, which would still raise the share of housing in average household income only to 10 percent. Rents would be indexed to inflation to keep them constant in real terms. Further rent increases are expected over the coming five years as the government has indicated rents should also cover major repairs (World Bank 1990). However, in July 1990, the Polish government decided to postpone the next (January) round of rent increases. So the implementation of this policy is unclear as of August 1990.

Tenants in both state- and cooperative-owned rental also benefit from low billing rates for central heating and hot water. These payments, made to heating companies in cities, accounted for a quarter of housing subsidies in 1989--2 percent of the central government budget. Tenants pay between only 10 and 25 percent of the true cost for providing these services (World Bank 1990). In contrast, households that do not have access to these services and rely on individual suppliers are not subsidized and pay full cost. Businesses and industries, even if linked to the central system, are required to pay full cost as well.

Like the maintenance subsidy, this support is regressive. The subsidy is granted to households without regard to income levels and households with larger units receive a larger benefit. In addition, the subsidy provides a strong disincentive to conserve heat or hot water--the more consumed, the greater the subsidy.

The reform of 1990 has apparently eliminated these subsidies. However, some price controls remain on coal and other energy supplies; it is not clear if the new prices for central heating and hot water reflect their "true" cost.

The government has set up an expanded "social aid" program to protect low-income households, such as pensioners, against the increases in rents and heating charges.

In conclusion, whereas the Polish government was exceptionally daring in undertaking overall economic reforms at the start of 1990, the changes in housing sector policies have been more limited with the exception of housing finance. And it appears that additional reforms of rents, for example, will be more difficult to effect than the reforms undertaken in January, at least in the short term. At the same time, the decentralization of responsibility for governmental actions for the development of new housing has been shifted to the local level, which may result in significant improvements over the next few years. Housing construction should also become more efficient as SOEs are forced to exist in a market environment. Nevertheless, although overall progress is being made and is likely to continue the task ahead remains formidable, despite the broad reforms of January.

Notes, chapter five

1. Unless otherwise noted, the data presented in this section is drawn from IMF (1989c).

2. Greater competition and freedom of operation has also been allowed with the foreign trade organizations (FTOs), as well as giving state enterprises easier access to foreign trade and investment. However, FTOs still accounted for over 90 percent of Polish trade in 1989 (IMF 1989c).

3. The law on privatization was passed in July 1990 and allows the Ministry of Ownership Transformation to select enterprises for privatization. (Five SOEs were chosen in the first month.) The Ministry will help the firms prepare proper accounts and value their assets. Following transformation into a joint stock company wholly owned by the government, the shares will be sold by auction, public offering, or negotiated purchase. Foreign share purchases of more than 10 percent will require ministerial approval. Workers will have preferential access to a fifth of the shares offered. However, regulations governing the operation of the securities markets and the supporting infrastructure for share trading still remain to be established.

4. Data in this section is from World Bank (1987) unless otherwise noted.

Chapter Six

THE HOUSING SECTOR IN CZECHOSLOVAKIA

Czechoslovakia's history of reform is marked by stops and starts, most notably the retrenchment after the "Prague Spring" of 1968. In the 20 years that followed, the economic system followed a modified form of the traditional CPE model, with five-year central plans and an emphasis on investment in heavy industry. Some planning devolved to the managers of VHJs (*vyrobne hospodarska jednotka*, similar to the *kombinats* found in other CPEs) and plan targets were refined in an attempt to shift the focus of SOE managers away from gross output and towards quality, productivity, and innovation.

These modest changes, however, were insufficient to ward off the structural problems inherent in the CPE. In 1981-82, triggered by a slump in foreign trade and rising external indebtedness, Czechoslovakia experienced an economic downturn. Though not as severe as the problems in neighboring Poland, the recession necessitated a radical revision of the economic plan and imposition of an austerity program to reduce foreign debt and cut imports.

Since 1985, policy makers have recognized that the country's economic problems could only be solved by reforming the economic system itself. The political changes of 1990 have accelerated the pace of reform, although Czechoslovakia is still taking a much more cautious approach to reform than Poland or Hungary, the region's keenest reformers. Reform is just beginning to affect housing, but the trend away from dominance of housing investment by the state and SOEs is already well-established. Development of a well-functioning housing sector will depend on the success of reforms that reduce the cost to society of producing housing (through direct grants and implicit price subsidies) and allow private producers to fill the gap left by the state and its agents.

DEMOGRAPHIC TRENDS

Czechoslovakia's population is currently about 15.6 million. Population decreased as a result of boundary contractions after World War II and has grown slowly in the post-war period, increasing by roughly one-third in the 30 years between 1950 and 1980. The growth rate eased in the 1980s and is now well below replacement level, though it will pick up again over the coming decade as an echo of the post-war baby boom is felt in the late 1990s (see table 6.1).

However, stability of the overall population masks the rapid expansion in Slovakia, a more rural, less industrialized region than the Czech Republic. The census shows that in the period from 1970 to 1980 the population in Slovakia increased 9.9 percent, compared to only 4.9 percent in the Czech Republic. This trend has persisted in the 1980s. Continued rapid population growth in Slovakia, with the higher rates of urbanization it is likely to experience as it develops, could have serious implications for housing, as shortages tend to be concentrated in urban areas.

Table 6.1   CZECHOSLOVAKIA--POPULATION TRENDS
1970-2000

	1970	1980	1990	2000
Total population (millions)	14.4	15.3	15.8	16.6
Percent of total				
Age 14 and under	23.1	24.3	23.1	21.3
Age 15-64	65.7	63.3	65.3	66.5
Age 65 and over	11.3	12.5	11.6	12.2
Dependency ratio[a] (percent)	52.3	58.1	53.2	50.4
Urban population (percent)	55.2	62.3	67.7	71.5
Annual growth (percent)				
Total	0.3	0.7	-0.3	0.5
Urban	1.8	1.7	1.0	1.0
Rural	-1.4	-0.9	-1.1	-0.6

Source: United Nations (1986).

a. The dependency ratio is the sum of the population under age 15 and age 65 and over divided by the population aged 15-64 expressed as a percentage.

Another important demographic tend is the declining average size of households over time, which increases the effective demand for housing for a given population level. Between 1960 and 1980, the number of single-person households doubled and the number of households with five or more persons fell by 50 percent. The average household size in 1980 was 2.8 persons, down from 3.1 in 1960.

ECONOMIC OVERVIEW[1]

In 1985, the Czechoslovak government recognized that the economy was suffering from many difficulties: industrial production was inefficient and wasteful of imported raw materials and energy; technical innovation was slow and goods produced did not meet world quality standards; productivity of assets had fallen every year since 1980; new investment projects took longer to complete, tying up capital and often becoming obsolete before they were completed; producers were unresponsive to consumer demand, creating stockpiles of unsalable goods and long-running shortages of foods that were in demand. The need for an overhaul of the system was clear, but it was not until 1987 and the advent of *perestroika* in the Soviet Union that significant changes could be contemplated openly.

The reforms planned for 1990 and later clearly intend to transform the Czechoslovak economy to one based on real markets and free prices. However, substantial conflict remains over how fast the changes should occur. Immediate transition, like the Polish "Big Bang", has been ruled out; a more gradual process, spread over several years, which would avoid the social costs of increased inflation and mass unemployment, is envisioned. The most important question facing the reformers is whether the government can afford the costs (in terms of maintaining subsidies) that go with the gradualist approach as the economy is opened up to competition.

State Enterprise Reform and the Private Sector

The outline of reform of carried out in 1987-89 centered on the state's production apparatus and was similar to that followed in Czechoslovakia in the 1960s (and elsewhere in Eastern Europe in the 1970s and 1980s): enterprise autonomy with self-financing and foreign trading rights; an end to centralized planning; breaking up large SOEs; increasing the scope for cooperatives and small private businesses.

Not surprisingly, the result was much the same as where these reforms had been tried elsewhere--little real change. The reorganization of industry in mid-1988, which created 2,778 SOEs from previously existing VHJs, did not establish a more competitive or flexible structure. In most cases, the new enterprises remained quite large (for example, the average firm in the garment industry employed 4,000 workers) and operated without competition in areas assigned to them by the planning bureaucracy.

Reforms of ownership forms and enterprise independence had similar fates. At the end of 1989, the economy was still dominated by SOEs. Changes to induce greater enterprise autonomy were undercut by intervention from central planners and management elections that offered no real choice to workers.

In 1990, more radical changes are under way. Three important reforms, which will displace SOEs from their past privileged positions, have been passed:

- *Private enterprise.* This law removes restrictions on private businesses, including the need for approval to establish a firm, its sphere of activity, and previous limits on the number of employees or capital involved. Firms may also sell shares to other parties, including foreign investors. Small businesses still face bureaucratic problems, though, such as the scarcity of premises for conducting business (which are controlled by local authorities).

- *Joint ventures.* Foreign investors can operate in Czechoslovakia under the same conditions as local firms. However, foreign firms still require a license to engage in foreign trade and repatriation of profits is dependent on hard currency earnings. (Internal convertibility of the koruna is not planned until January 1991.)

- *Privatization of SOEs.* An Office of State Enterprise and Privatization was established in the Ministry of Finance in April. It plans to carry out the sale of SOEs in two stages. First, enterprises will be evaluated and turned into joint stock companies. A proportion (about one-fifth) of these shares would be pooled in national unit trust and distributed to the population. The second stage, sale of the rest of the shares, is not planned until early 1991.

Financial System

The prewar Czechoslovakian financial system had been sophisticated, with a central bank, commercial banks, smaller local banks and financial intermediaries--insurance companies, investment houses, and brokerage firms. The post-war Czechoslovak banking system was restructured to provide the investment, distribution, and monitoring network needed in a CPE: a central bank (Statni State Bank), an investment bank (Investicni), a foreign operations bank, a commercial bank (created from nationalized banks), and state savings banks in each of the two republics. Under this system, banks merely acted as a means of channelling the credit needed by SOEs to fulfill their plan targets.

In January 1990 this monolithic banking system was dismantled. The central bank was stripped of its five commercial divisions and will henceforth be involved only in traditional central bank activities--implementing monetary policies (e.g., interest rates and the money supply) and regulating banking institutions.

Commercial operations are to be conducted by two state-owned banks created at the same time. (Two regional savings banks were also established.) The two new commercial banks have been given wide latitude to develop their own business (including foreign transactions such as bond placements for local businesses) and make loans on a commercial basis to SOEs. The main source of funds for the commercial banks will be a discount facility established by central bank. Set at 4 percent (just above current inflation of 3 percent), the discount rate establishes the first benchmark in the credit system. However, interest rate controls remain in place until the system of price subsidies is overhauled. The banks are also authorized to raise capital through bond issues.

The investment bank will continue to lend for long-term projects, such as housing. Given the bank's freedom to operate on a commercial basis, it seems inevitable that many projects will require state subsidies to attract financing. However, this will be an important change: the government will have to recognize the cost explicitly in its budget rather than implicitly through a loss to the bank.

Prices and Fiscal Policy

The price reform of 1989, which used centrally set wholesale prices to attempt to equalize the return on SOEs' fixed assets, failed to achieve its aim. SOEs were able to provide biased information and raise their actual returns. The result was increased demand for financial support on the part of some SOEs and increased surpluses (which the government could not recoup) for others. More radical measures were required if prices were to provide real information about scarcity and demand. In addition, the price reform had induced inflationary pressure and was putting upward pressure on spending for subsidies.

A fundamental tenet of the Czechoslovak reform process is to avoid the inflationary blast that gripped Poland in the late 1980s. The notion is to create competition before eliminating price controls; the competition would then restrain inflation. The 1990 reform plan aims to gradually remove price controls, first at the industrial level and second at the retail level. Subsidies amounting to CsK28 billion ($1.6 billion) annually are to be cut during 1990 in order to eliminate the budget deficit and move towards freeing prices, with all price controls lifted by 1992.

However, as with the pace of reform in general, there remains conflict over how quickly to unleash the full impact of the price rises. To soften the blow caused by the price increases, monthly compensatory payments of CsK140 ($8.20)--about 4 percent of the average monthly wage--are to be added to all wages until 1991. To keep wage rises from triggering an inflationary spiral, legislation is planned to impose a stiff tax penalty on companies that give wage increases above a 3 percent guideline.

Although the budget will show a surplus in 1990, it is not the level of the deficit that matters in Czechoslovakia, as was the case in Poland, as much as what public sector funds are used for. (Budgets had been balanced through most of the 1970s and 1980s.) The pattern in the past was to use subsidies to shield the domestic economy from having to adapt to changing conditions. Cuts in subsidies are necessary to reverse this trend: reductions of between 2 and 5 percent for urban transport, housing, and domestic heating; cuts of more than 10 percent for SOEs, agriculture, and mining. To counter public fears, spending on health and social welfare has been increased. The danger Czechoslovakia faces is the possible instability caused by the continual adjustment of prices and counter-measures to cushion the impact of price changes (i.e., wage increases and subsidies). Similar approaches have been tried in Poland, Yugoslavia, and Hungary, with poor results. Half-hearted reforms in these countries succeeded only in making the existing situation worse. Through mid-1990, Czechoslovakia's cautious course of reform has continued the country's steady (but unspectacular) performance of the 1980s. (Table 6.2 gives some economic indicators and a forecast of future results.) It remains to be seen if Czechoslovakia can find a gradual strategy that works. If so, it will be the exception in Eastern Europe.

THE HOUSING SECTOR

The housing sector in Czechoslovakia faces problems similar to those found in other centrally planned economies (CPEs): an inability to overcome persistent housing deficits; declining productivity and production that cannot adapt to changing household demand; and large subsidies for both home purchase and rental units. To date, only minor reforms have touched the housing sector.

In terms of scale relative to the overall economy, the housing sector in Czechoslovakia is one of the smallest in Eastern Europe. In the 1980s, housing investment in the country fell from 4.4 percent of NMP in 1980 to 3.4 percent of NMP in 1987. Only the German Democratic Republic and Romania showed lower levels of activity. On the investment side, Czechoslovakia ranks about in the middle of East European countries. Investment in housing represented 12.5 percent of total investment in 1985 (down from 13.2 percent in 1980), about half the level in Poland and Hungary, but also about 50 percent higher than in Romania. By 1987, housing's share in total investment had declined further to 11.9 percent.[2]

In 1985, housing accounted for about one-third of the output of the construction sector, which made up 10.9 percent of NMP (EIU, 1989c). This reflected the Czechoslovak government strategy of continued heavy investment in industry. Productivity in the sector, based on the number of units constructed and the real flow of resources into the housing sector, has fallen by about 21 percent during 1980-85. One explanation for the fall in productivity is the steady flow of skilled labor out of the construction sector and into sectors given priority by the government and paying higher wages (such as chemicals and nonferrous metals).

Housing Stock and Production

The 1980 census of housing registered 4.9 million occupied dwellings in Czechoslovakia (ECE Committee 1987). The average age of the housing stock was 34.5 years--down from the 45.5 years recorded in 1970 as a result of the high levels of production in the early 1970s. Ownership of housing in 1980 was about evenly split between individual owners and public sector owners (such as local housing authorities--known as National Committees--and state-sponsored cooperatives); 49.7 percent and 50.2 percent, respectively.[3] The composition of the stock is also about evenly split between small (one- and two-family) units (49.5 percent) and multi-family dwellings (50.5 percent).

Table 6.2   ECONOMIC INDICATORS 1986-90 (Percentage change at constant prices)

	1986	1987	1988	1989[b]	1990[c]
GDP	2.6	2.2	2.9	1.9	0.5
Retail prices	0.5	0.1	0.3	1.4	7.0
Current account[a] ($ millions)	200	-280	-320	-150	-300

Source: EUI (1990).

a. Trade in convertible currencies only.
b. Estimated.
c. Projected.

Annual housing production (new construction) has declined relentlessly since 1975, when the state sector constructed 144,700 units (Miskiewicz 1986). In 1985, total annual production was 104,400 units and by 1988 it had fallen to 82,900 units. By any measure, this is very low: the 1988 level represents only 1.4 percent of the housing stock (at that time) of 5.9 million units.

The combination of declining housing production, a high loss rate in the housing stock, an increasing rate of household formation, and a shrinking average household size implies that the housing shortage is probably getting worse. In 1985, annual production accounted for only two thirds the number of new households formed (through marriage and divorce) in Czechoslovakia (United Nations 1988). Another factor adding pressure on the housing sector is the increase in money incomes of most households, which creates increased interest in home-ownership and adds to the demand for higher quality units.

The 1980 census reported that the number of households exceeded the number of existing housing units (both inhabited and uninhabited) by 98,000. However, this simple measure understates the actual shortage. In terms of occupied units, the number of households without dwellings of their own is 466,000 (ECE Committee 1987). The difference is explained mainly by a geographic mismatch between households and the housing stock. In rural areas, the number of dwellings is more than sufficient; in urban areas (especially large towns and industrial centers), the housing shortage is acute. The expansion of the housing stock in urban areas is also hindered by a shortage of capacity and investment funds for the expansion of central heating systems and water supply.

The average waiting time for a unit in 1985 was about five years (United Nations 1988); this has probably lengthened with lower levels of production. Worse, the shortfall in housing production is understated by the previous measures, since it does not take into account the very high rate of demolition and retirement of units from the stock nor the high level of substandard units. In 1986, it was estimated that about 20,000 units were lost annually and that a total of 220,000 were either in such poor condition as to be uninhabitable or were slated for demolition.

Overall trends indicate improved levels of quality in housing--a rise in the average floor space per unit from 39.2 square meters in 1970 to 43.8 square meters in 1980; a fall in the average number of occupants per unit from 3.4 to 3.1 during the same time period; and a rise in the proportion of units with three or more rooms (not including kitchens and bathrooms) from 30.6 percent in 1970 to 45.8 percent in 1980. However, a large share of the housing stock is crowded and lacks basic amenities. The 1980 census reported that over 40 percent of households had less than 8 square meters of floor space per person and 1.2 million units (about one-quarter of the stock) had no toilet facilities within the unit. In addition, many large-scale housing developments have been constructed in recent years without sufficient supporting infrastructure. In Bratislava, for example, dormitory communities have been constructed that house over 100,000 persons but lack adequate transport and roads, health clinics, and shopping facilities (Miskiewicz 1986).

Construction and Building Materials Industry

Housing production in Czechoslovakia, like most other East European countries, is split between the state, state-owned enterprises (SOEs), cooperatives, and private individuals. Up to the mid-1970s, the state and state enterprises played the dominant investment role in the housing sector, relying exclusively on construction SOEs to carry out their projects. Since that time, emphasis has been shifting away from SOEs and towards cooperatives, both as investors and builders.[4] (In fact, SOEs have not been permitted to develop housing on their own account since 1981, although projects started before that date have been allowed to proceed to completion.) The state construction enterprises now build units for the state housing authorities and under contract with cooperatives. SOEs' share of production has fallen from 24 percent in 1975 to 2 percent in 1988. In the same period, the share of production by cooperatives rose from 27 percent to 44 percent. Production by private households has edged up slightly during this time, from 21 percent to 27 percent of the total (United Nations 1989a).

A total of 65 SOEs, ranging in size from 100 to 9,000 employees and controlled by the Ministry of Building Construction, accounted for 62 percent of all building construction work carried out in 1985 (ECE Committee 1987). About 90 percent of housing built by SOEs uses prefabricated, large-panel construction technology. As in other CPEs where this method is used, this approach requires that state-built housing be developed near the prefabrication factories and that several hundred (or more) units be constructed on a single large site to capture the technology's economies of scale. (Some experiments have been tried to change from concrete-based prefabrication systems to wood-based panels, which would allow a smaller economic scale of construction and utilize a local resource. To date, no widespread application has been developed.)

These prefabricated concrete systems have not been effective in Czechoslovakia in achieving their scale economies or producing housing that meets household demand. The SOEs do not face suitable incentives for the timely completion of projects or adequate quality control. Poor quality components require expensive and labor-intensive on-site repair and finishing work to complete construction of the units. Households complain that the units do not respond to their needs (particularly with respect to amenities such as heating and ventilation).

State construction enterprises have also been unable to meet the need for repair and rehabilitation of the state housing stock (arising from the initial low quality of construction and the neglect of maintenance). SOEs lack the technical equipment, skilled craftsmen, and materials required to carry out these functions.

In 1982, cooperatives counted just over 1 million members and had produced about 700,000 units (or 15 percent of the housing stock). Cooperatives are established in one of two forms, depending on the program under which they develop their housing: (1) "stabilization" housing; and (2) "self-help" housing. Cooperatives producing stabilization housing were created as part of government policy changes in 1982, which called for cooperatives to replace enterprises as developers of housing, mainly because of misallocation and speculation in SOE-produced housing. These cooperatives are linked with particular industries or SOEs and require their members to fulfill certain conditions to qualify for a housing unit. These conditions include: an obligation to remain with the SOE for a period of 10 to 15 years; a requirement that the recipient occupy the dwelling, which cannot be sold or have the rights transferred (except under certain conditions); and repayment of home purchase grants by the SOE if the member's work contract is cancelled.

The self-help form of cooperatives is open to wider membership, but requires members to finance part of the construction costs through a deposit and to agree to provide between 2,500 and 3,000 hours of work to the cooperative on the construction site. These cooperatives have improved the performance of the housing delivery system, particularly for households that have difficulty qualifying or cannot wait for state housing; a young couple can often obtain a unit from a self-help cooperative within two to three years (Blaha 1984). However, these cooperatives, because of their decentralized nature, difficulties with access to materials, and bureaucratic opposition, have not yet been able to prove themselves as efficient housing producers.

Private construction firms apparently account for only a small part of officially recorded construction activity (by value). Official statistics state that almost all construction activity outside SOEs is carried out by other construction units controlled by central government ministries, local government, or cooperative building corporations. However, because more than a quarter of annual housing production is undertaken by private individuals who are unlikely to contract with a state construction enterprise or cooperative, significant private construction capacity must exist. It seems likely that private construction activity is small in scale and either is confined to the "second" economy outside the control of the central planning apparatus or takes the form of household self-help (although no source explicitly mentions self-help construction as an important approach outside the context of cooperatives).

Construction sponsored by private individuals remains a significant proportion of construction, but has not been a readily available alternative for most of the population. Labor and building materials are often in short supply. Although the law allows households to "borrow" construction equipment (while paying for costs associated with its use) from SOEs as long as the enterprise's production activities were not hindered, in practice this has been difficult. The law also provides for local authorities to "guarantee" access by households building units privately to 23 basic building materials, though it is not clear how well this program has functioned (Blaha 1984).

Housing Allocation and Tenure

Rental units in state-owned blocks are intended to be assigned to the most socially disadvantaged citizens, but misallocation of these flats has been widespread (Pisova 1990). Since 1966, the Czechoslovak government has made state rental housing available for sale, although it was not until 1978 that sales could go ahead without the concurrence of all tenants in the building. In 1984, the most prized apartments in city centers (though often lacking modern comforts) were selling for CsK100,000 (about $15,000).[5] More modern units of moderate size (about 2 to 3 rooms), in better condition, sold for CsK200,000 ($30,000). Of course, demand always far exceeded supply.[6]

Czechoslovakia has permitted individual ownership of homes and apartments. An individual can own one residence and one vacation home. Owners can buy and sell homes in the private market. Land for private housing construction has been available from both local authorities and private landowners. Land (up to 800 square meters) could be purchased from the state at a cost ranging from CsK4 to CsK15 ($0.60 to $2.30) per square meter, depending on the location. About a third of private housing constructed in 1983 was built on land obtained--apparently on a free-market basis--from private landowners or on family-owned land (Blaha 1984).

Housing Finance

RENTAL HOUSING

Flats constructed by the state are financed entirely out of the government budget. In 1985, government outlays to support state-sector construction of housing and supporting residential infrastructure totalled CsK14.5 billion--2.6 percent of NMP (ECE Committee 1987). Rents in state and enterprise housing are fixed according to floor area and amenities (but not location) and have not been changed since 1964. Further progressive rent reductions ranging from 5 to 50 percent are available depending on the number of children in the household. Additional rent subsidies are also provided to students, apprentices, the elderly, and disabled persons.

Low rents and ineffective management of state housing has forced the government to provide funds to subsidize operating expenses. About 60 percent of all recurrent costs for state rental housing are funded out of the state budget (Pisova 1990). These subsidies represent 20 percent of all public sector on-budget spending on housing and were equal to 1.0 percent of NMP in 1985 (ECE Committee 1987).

Despite these subsidies, most blocks of flats are in poor condition as public funding for the housing sector was mainly devoted to new construction, neglecting repair and maintenance. In addition, shortages of necessary building materials and skilled craftsmen have also contributed to the decline in social housing conditions. It is currently estimated that CsK30 billion ($1.8 billion or about 4.9 percent of 1989 NMP) is required for necessary repairs to the state-owned housing stock (Pisova 1990). This repair bill is likely to climb over time as further defects emerge in recently constructed blocks that use prefabrication technology.

FINANCE FOR HOME PURCHASE

As part of the shift in policy away from state-provided housing, programs were adopted to provide subsidies in order to induce families to build houses through cooperatives or on their own. In 1985, about CsK6.1 billion (1.1 percent of NMP) was spent on direct capital subsidies supporting cooperative and individual housing construction. (Indirect subsidies provided through very low-interest mortgages have not been estimated.)

Subsidy programs were offered based on the purchase price and a sliding need-based scale (Pisova 1990):

- *Private construction:* 40-year loan at 2.7 percent annual interest from state bank (with 10 years grace) for CsK120,000 (about $7,700 in 1989), about 30 percent of the cost of an average unit;

- *Cooperatives:* 40 to 50 percent of construction cost financed through 40-year loan at 1.0 percent annual interest loan from the state--cooperative members agree to provide between 2,500 and 3,000 hours of work for the cooperative on the housing site.

In addition, employees of SOEs in priority sectors may qualify for additional support in the purchase of a cooperative housing unit or interest-free loans for housing built by the SOE itself. Subsidized loans are available for up to 100 percent of the construction cost for workers in nuclear and nonferrous metal industries. Workers in other industries, such as heavy chemicals, ceramics and glass, and metallurgy, can receive subsidized loans for up to 75 percent of the cost of the unit (Blaha 1984).

Beyond these subsidies, other lending for housing in the past has been offered through institutions such as the Slovenska State Savings Bank (similar to a savings and loan institution). The banks' main function was to hold household savings and to lend to individuals and small enterprises. However, the mortgages carried low fixed interest rates and were made available without using risk premia or price-based rationing to discriminate among potential borrowers.

These extensive subsidies mean that households, on average, devote a very small part of their net disposable income to housing. A 1985 survey found that industrial workers spent only 2.1 percent of their income on housing (rent or loan repayments). A further 5.1 percent is spent on utilities, such as water, heat, electricity, gas (ECE Committee 1987).

Future Directions in Housing Reforms

Czechoslovakia currently lags behind Poland and Hungary in its reform process. However, discussions are now under way to develop a new housing policy that addresses some of the problems facing the sector. Pisova (1990) reports that, unlike Poland, Czechoslovakia is likely to follow a gradualist approach, with the transition period lasting through 1993-95. Key areas of reform will include:

- Redefined property relations allowing additional forms of property ownership and leasehold with considerations for tenant rights;

- Reform of public sector financing for the housing sector, including rents, operating subsidies, and lending;

- Privatization of both housing and the construction industry.

Notes, chapter six

1. Unless otherwise indicated economic data are from EIU (various).

2. Data for 1980-85 are from United Nations (1988); figures for 1987 are from United Nations (1989a).

3. The remaining 0.1 percent are owned by foreign citizens and other non-state organizations.

4. In Czechoslovakia, cooperatives may act either as a developer (contracting with a SOE to provide construction services) or a developer/constructor (whereby the cooperative undertakes the construction work itself without reliance on state construction enterprises or private firms). Most cooperatives are apparently organized primarily as construction units which members join in order to gain improved access to housing (i.e., the queue is shorter than

for state rental housing but the household bears a larger share of the costs).

5. US dollar equivalents are given based on the official exchange rate for the year quoted.

6. Blaha (1984) is unclear as to whether these are market-driven or administratively-set prices.

Chapter Seven

THE HOUSING SECTOR IN YUGOSLAVIA

Among the CPEs of Eastern Europe, Yugoslavia was a pioneer of economic reform. Since the 1950s, it has been facing up to the types of questions now being asked in Poland, Hungary, and other countries. In some regards, Yugoslavia seemed to take the right steps to fashion a more market-oriented economy: central planning was abolished; foreign investors were welcome. However, in many other senses, the country's reforms only went half way: spending was never fully subjected to the rigors of the market; bureaucrats with little commercial experience were allowed to make major decisions over the allocation of resources. As a result, the economic growth which propelled Yugoslavia past its Eastern European counterparts in the 1960s and 1970s has come to a near standstill.

The Yugoslav reforms, described in more detail below, provide several lessons on how economic reform should be approached. Perhaps the most important message is that attempting to maintain a compromise between a market economy and a CPE is difficult--a conclusion with which reformers in Hungary and Poland would agree and which underlines the potential danger of the slow reform routes being favored by Bulgaria, Czechoslovakia, and Romania.

The Yugoslav reform experience underlines one other major lesson: the financial sector is key to successful reform. Yugoslavia never suffered from a shortage of capital, but rather from its easy terms and unproductive use. More than half of its $20 billion debt was used to subsidize consumption and fund projects which provided no real return (Forman 1990). The borrowing helped to subsidize economic half-steps which did not lead to long-term improvement in the functioning of the economy. Thus, the Yugoslav experience indicates developing a financial system that imposes market discipline free of bureaucratic interference is a necessary condition for successful reform, no matter how much legal and administrative reform is undertaken.

These lessons are not only valuable examples for the other reforming countries of the region, but have also prompted a more critical examination of past reforms by the Yugoslavs themselves. As a result, 1989 and 1990 have seen the country embark on its most radical reforms yet.

DEMOGRAPHIC TRENDS

Yugoslavia's population is about 24 million. Population growth has declined to an annual rate of about 0.6 percent in the 1980s from a rate of 1.1 percent in the period 1953 to 1983. The decline in population growth has been mainly a result of decline in the birth rate, which fell by over 15 percent between 1965 and 1990. While this has led to a declining share of persons under 14 years of age in the population, improvements in life expectancy have raised the share of the elderly in the population as a whole (see table 7.1). Thus, the dependency ratio will begin to rise, putting greater demand on social services associated with the elderly.

Table 7.1 YUGOSLAVIA--POPULATION TRENDS 1970-2000

	1970	1980	1990	2000
Total population (millions)	20.3	22.3	23.9	25.2
Percent of total				
Age 14 and under	27.4	24.8	22.8	20.5
Age 15-64	64.8	66.2	68.0	66.9
Age 65 and over	7.8	9.0	9.2	12.6
Dependency ratio[a] (percent)	54.4	51.0	47.1	49.5
Urban population (percent)	34.8	42.3	50.2	57.5
Annual growth (percent)				
Total	0.9	0.9	0.6	0.5
Urban	3.1	2.8	2.3	1.8
Rural	-0.1	-0.4	-0.9	-1.1

Source: United Nations (1986).

a. The dependency ratio is the sum of the population under age 15 and age 65 and over divided by the population age 15-64 expressed as a percentage.

The country has become more urbanized over the past 30 years. The urban share of total population almost doubled from 28 percent in 1960 to 50 percent in 1990. (Even so, this level of urbanization ranks Yugoslavia as one of the least urbanized countries in Europe.) Rising urbanization is the result of Yugoslavia's focus on industrial development in the post-war era: the number of persons involved in agriculture fell from 50 percent of the population in 1961 to only 19 percent in 1981; low agricultural prices and subsidized rents encouraged migration to urban areas.[1] Urban growth rates have been declining steadily from the high rates of the 1950s and 1960s, but rural areas continue to lose population at an increasing rate. These shifts will continue to put pressure on urban housing.

OVERVIEW OF ECONOMIC REFORM[2]

The break with other CPEs in Eastern Europe and the Soviet Union in 1949 sent Yugoslavia down its unique road of economic development. Following a brief attempt to impose even greater central control, decentralization was rapidly embraced: state enterprises were (theoretically) handed over to their workers and self-management adopted; central planning was abandoned in 1952; collectivization was halted and even reversed beginning in 1953.

Reforms in the 1960s extended legislative independence to Yugoslavia's constituent republics and gave greater autonomy to regional levels of government (communes). Reforms to move the economy toward a freer market orientation were also undertaken in the 1960s and 1970s. The result has been weak economic control by central government. Most planning takes place at the enterprise level, with negotiations between different enterprises setting production levels and driving pricing decisions. Yugoslavia's current reform initiatives (spurred by the need to borrow from the World Bank and IMF and meet its debt service obligations) favor increasing private economic activity, rationalizing the price structure, and reducing the influence of SOEs.

State Enterprises and the Private Sector

Self-management has been the keystone of the Yugoslavian version of the socialized economy. In theory, the workers in an enterprise (also know in Yugoslavia as a "social organization") elect their own managers and approve their annual plan (with only a general reference to the national plan). In practice, self-management has meant that the enterprise has to be run on the basis of a broad consensus, making it virtually impossible to make workers redundant or close down an enterprise. The security of job tenure ensured by self-management has also brought problems that undermined the viability of the system and necessitated more radical reforms.

Relying mainly on a program of macroeconomic measures, such as making the dinar convertible to inject foreign competition in the economy and tight monetary policy (along the lines of the Polish reform program), the latest reforms are an attempt to remove the ability of enterprises to drive up prices unilaterally. The program has succeeded in halting inflation (which had been running at an annual rate of 2,500 percent at the end of 1989), but so far unemployment has not risen sharply.

This is because the financial system has still been very accommodating to enterprises' borrowing needs, and real interest rates only became positive at the beginning of 1990. Although the government is not intentionally subsidizing unhealthy enterprises, heavily indebted (and probably unviable) enterprises continue to receive financing at the same time as more successful enterprises lack the funds and incentives to invest.

The next step in reform will attempt to bring more discipline to bear on the enterprises, by allowing self-managing enterprises to sell equity stakes to individual and foreign investors and by tightening the flow of credit. It is expected that such changes will cause a wave of bankruptcies, with 300,000 job losses pushing the unemployment rate up to 14 percent (1.5 million unemployed).

Financial and Banking System

Yugoslavia's banking and financial system is unlike that of the other Eastern European countries. Yugoslavia's banking system has, as in other CPEs, served as a financial intermediary to facilitate enterprise operations, but it is similar to Western banking in that the commercial ("basic") banks are not state-owned. Basic banks are owned by "founders." Yugoslavian enterprises can create banks with their own capital. Worker councils also manage and own banks.

Because the banks are in practice subservient to their founders, the commercial banks are underdeveloped, overly decentralized, and very inefficient. In 1983, there were over 400 banks in Yugoslavia (Golijanin 1984). Despite these numbers, there is almost no competition between banks over deposit taking or loans, since each bank's set of founders provide a fixed clientele. With the negative real interest rates that have prevailed over the past 20 years, these "captive" banks have had little incentive to evaluate and judge investment projects on tough economic criteria. The result has been easily available financing and a country littered with unproductive investments.

A central bank, the National Bank of Yugoslavia, previously operated as the main instrument for financing government deficits. Because the government is forbidden by law to have a deficit, the central bank was required to finance government shortfalls through either expansion of the money supply or increasing reserve requirements for the commercial banks. (With reserve requirements running as high as 25 percent on banks' loan portfolios and paying interest at only a fraction of the banks' cost of funds, the effect of the reserve requirements was to transfer the government's debts to the commercial banks.) The central bank also started operating as a commercial bank, taking deposits and making loans, in order to cover the losses it was carrying from the government's debts.

In 1989, reforms were implemented to transform the central bank into an institution that operates along Western lines (i.e., manages monetary policy, controls foreign exchange rates and balances, and supervises other banks). Real interest rates have been made positive, but the fundamental problems with the commercial banks have yet to be addressed. For example, the central bank is no longer required to assist basic banks that have over-extended themselves, but unless the government is willing to let banks as well as enterprises go bankrupt, the banks will continue to support the enterprises to which they are linked.

One indicator of the underdevelopment of the financial system is that enterprises are currently 80 percent self-financing. To a degree this reflects the lack of an adequate capital market. The self-funding is an indication that many enterprises could not pay a market interest rate. Self-funding also makes the central bank's task of controlling the money supply more difficult.

Prices

Beginning in 1979 prices were gradually freed from administrative controls and many prices were market determined; by 1989, 85 percent of all prices were free of administrative control. However, inflation increased steadily throughout the 1980s, reaching 76 percent in 1985 and 180 percent in 1988. Despite widespread controls on prices and wages, hyperinflation attacked the economy until more fundamental reforms were instituted in 1990. With the dinar made convertible and effectively pegged to the Deutschemark, inflation came to a practical halt by April 1990. The government has set a goal to end price controls by the end of 1990.

THE HOUSING SECTOR[3]

Although Yugoslavia has achieved impressive improvements in average dwelling quality (better materials, more amenities, and more floor space per occupant) since 1945, the housing sector still demonstrates shortcomings that are all too familiar in Eastern Europe--declining levels of production and increasing housing shortages. The structural housing shortage problem associated with centralized control of production was aggravated by other factors: high levels of migration from rural areas (driven by depressed prices for agricultural products and low-cost social housing); weaknesses in town planning and production of serviced land; almost nonexistent cost recovery from the social housing stock. Recent changes in housing policy in Yugoslavia have sought to reverse its previous emphasis, so that housing construction and maintenance moves from being primarily a responsibility of the state to one which clearly belongs to the household.

The share of housing (which includes utilities in the Yugoslav national accounts) in national income has fallen dramatically since 1977, declining from 7.9 percent of GDP to 3.6 percent in 1985. This fall mirrors the overall decline of the share of investment in national income (from 33.1 percent of GDP in 1976 to 20.5 percent in 1985). Housing's share of total investment has also fallen, dropping from 24 percent in 1977 to 17 percent in 1985. The decline in the shares of housing investment was mainly a result of cuts in public sector investment: the number of social dwellings built in 1987 was down by 20,000 compared to 1980 (United Nations 1989a).

Housing and utilities account for about two-thirds of the output of the construction sector--which made up 6.9 percent of GDP in 1985 (United Nations 1989b). This is one of the highest shares in Eastern Europe and reflects the decentralization strategy Yugoslavia has pursued. Unlike other CPEs, which have cut housing investment to pour even more resources into "productive" sectors in an attempt to prop up economic growth, Yugoslavia has almost given up central direction of investment. This has caused significant problems (such as loss of control over credit), but it has allowed investment to be more strongly demand-driven.

Housing Stock and Production

Results from the 1981 census indicated that Yugoslavia had 6.1 million dwelling units, about evenly distributed between rural and urban areas. Overall, about one-fifth of all housing was in social ownership, the remainder owned privately. The rate of private ownership was much higher in rural areas (94 percent) than in urban areas (59 percent). The rental stock was held by both public and private owners: the 1.3 million social housing units plus an additional 525,000 housing units in private hands. Information on the average age of the housing stock is not available, but the norm for Eastern Europe is between 30 and 35 years. We do know that 77 percent of Yugoslavia's housing stock was built after World War II.

Despite the gains made since 1945 and the relative modernity of the housing stock, much housing is still considered inadequate, especially in terms of facilities:

> Less than 60 per cent of the dwellings are completely equipped, while nearly 4 per cent or almost 220,000 dwellings have no public utility installations whatsoever. Bathrooms are found in a little over half of the dwellings, and flush toilets in less than half. About 17 per cent of dwellings are in buildings which are not made of hard material (Popovic 1988).

The quality of housing also varies a great deal among the republics and autonomous provinces. For example, 86 percent of the units in Slovenia were fully equipped compared to only 29 percent of the units in Kosovo. In general, dwellings in rural areas (despite being newer on average because of heavy investment activity in the less-developed regions of the country) are more poorly equipped and have fewer facilities than those in urban settlements. Furthermore, housing quality is positively correlated with a region's level of economic and social development.

Other housing quality measures have shown steady improvement during the post-war period (including the 1980s). Between 1971 and 1987, the average dwelling floor space increased from 49.6 to 74.5 square meters, the number of persons per dwelling fell from 4.1 to 3.4, and the average floor space per person rose from 12.2 to 21.9 square meters.

Corresponding to the decrease in housing investment noted above was a decrease in the number of dwellings built. About 140,000 units per year were built during the late 1970s and early 1980s. During the mid-1980s production was about 130,000 units per year, and, in 1987, production fell sharply to 120,000 units per year (United Nations 1989a).

Unlike other CPEs, the decline in housing production in Yugoslavia cannot be traced to falling productivity in the construction sector. In fact, labor productivity in housing construction remained constant during 1980-85 and overall productivity (in terms of number of dwellings produced per unit of real resources invested) improved by about 50 percent. Although more detailed data are not available, it seems probable that some of these improvements are the result of greater private sector participation in housing production: the private sector share of housing investment (by value) increased from 50 percent in 1976 to around 66 percent in 1985; the private share of total production showed similar gains, rising from 59 percent to 67 percent during the same period.

However, although productivity gains indicate that Yugoslavia's incremental approach to economic reform may be starting to pay off, the falling levels of production are contributing to a worsening housing shortage. The 1981 census estimated the overall shortage of housing units in Yugoslavia to be 66,000 units. With an average of 3.5 persons per unit, this seems to imply that only 1 percent of Yugoslavia's population is affected by the housing deficit. However, these overall numbers mask more serious housing shortages.

The heavy rural-urban migration Yugoslavia experienced in the post-war era has produced severe shortages of housing in urban areas, especially in the larger cities, while creating an excess supply in some rural areas. (Most of the 206,000 vacant units identified in the 1981 census were concentrated in rural areas.) In fact, the housing deficit in urban areas totalled 195,000 dwellings in 1981. Sagging production through the 1980s has almost certainly increased this deficit. For example, gross production of housing in 1985 amounted to only 79 percent of the number of new households formed through marriage (Europa 1989); the shortfall is obviously larger when new households formed by divorce are considered.

The shortage of housing also manifests itself through overcrowding in existing housing. Using an adequacy criterion of one person per room, about 35 percent of all dwellings were overcrowded. In 1981, there was an average of 16.3 square meters of floor space per person; even so, over 6.6 million people (29 percent of the total population) lived in dwellings with less than 10 square meters of floor space per person. One indication of the severity of the shortage is that over 67,000 nonresidential structures were being used as dwellings in 1981.

Yugoslavia is near the bottom of the ranking of European countries according to the number of dwelling units per thousand inhabitants. In 1987, Yugoslavia had 300 dwellings per thousand residents (slightly more than Poland's 292). In comparison, Bulgaria, Czechoslovakia, and Hungary, all had measures greater than 360 (United Nations 1989a).

Construction and Building Materials Industry

Housing production in Yugoslavia is split primarily into two spheres--state-owned enterprises (SOEs, also known as work organizations or organizations of associated labor) and private individuals. The two types of producers operate under completely different conditions.[4] Until recently, SOEs have mainly produced large housing complexes using industrial construction technology, with little capacity to maintain or rehabilitate existing units, or to build single-family homes. SOEs built housing, usually under a soft budget constraint, for state housing authorities (called housing communities in Yugoslavia).[5] And, as in other CPEs, SOEs have consistently been the target of complaints about the quality of their construction, low productivity, and inability to complete units on time and on budget.

In contrast, individual households building their own dwellings relied mainly on their own financing and effort. This approach, which stretched out construction periods and raised costs, still represented a viable solution to households who could not satisfy their housing demand (either in terms of simple access to housing or in terms of housing type) in the social sector.

Since the mid-1970s, housing production has been shifting away from SOEs and toward the private sector: SOEs' share of production fell from 41 percent in 1976 to 32 percent in 1987 (United Nations 1989a). About 90 percent of the balance of housing production is undertaken and financed by private individuals. Cooperatives accounted for only 12 percent of all non-social housing (i.e., not sponsored by the state or SOEs) built during 1981-85.

Yugoslavia has a relatively large number of construction firms, almost all being SOEs. In 1987, there were 2,760 building firms employing 597,000 persons. Because of the policy of decentralization and self-management, state construction firms are generally smaller than in other Eastern European CPEs; 51 percent of the firms have between 61 and 500 employees. There are 87 firms with more than 1,000 employees, averaging 1,800 workers each. In comparison, in 1987, Bulgaria (with a third of Yugoslavia's population) has 74 construction SOEs with more than 1,000 employees, averaging 3,500 persons each (United Nations 1989a).

As was noted at the beginning of this section on the housing sector, the Yugoslav government has been encouraging a shift of housing production from the state sector to the private sector. The first step in this reform was included in the 1974 Constitution, which provided that the housing sector should be organized according to the principles of decentralization and self-management in order to achieve greater efficiency in housing production. The results, however, were quite the opposite.

Prices and construction periods increased rapidly as the SOEs, which were contracted to build the housing for the local housing authorities, still retained their monopoly over new construction and maintenance. The construction SOEs, faced with excess capacity brought about by declining economic activity and needing to keep their work force occupied, tended to stretch out the completion of housing projects as long as possible. Housing authorities had little incentive to control costs, since they received funding on easy terms from the central government.

In 1986, to try to inject some market discipline into SOE performance, the Yugoslav government authorized construction of 30,000 dwellings for sale at market prices. However, response to this initiative has been poor--construction companies lack the working capital to finance their own developments and households are unwilling to finance construction with their own savings or expensive, unsubsidized credit.

Since 1988, when hard budget constraints were imposed on SOEs, the home construction industry has contracted substantially; employment was down 5 percent in 1988. The contraction hits the construction SOEs on two fronts: (1) with loss-making SOEs now allowed to fail, weak construction SOEs face the possibility of closure; and (2) other SOEs no longer have easy access to funds for housing construction, as the government has stripped the welfare functions that previously justified the SOE role as housing investor.

There is little information available on how private individuals produce their own housing. Simoneti (1990) states that a large proportion of private housing is constructed through self-help. While some households are able to obtain credits for home building, most have to finance construction out of their own resources (see the discussion on the use of remittances to finance housing, below). In addition to problems regarding the acquisition of materials and skilled labor needed to complete a private dwelling, households face great difficulties in even securing a site upon which to build.

Due to the shortage of building lots, construction by private individuals without planning approval or permission to build is widespread in urban areas. The shortage is mainly a reflection of a town planning process which greatly underestimated the demand for lots to accommodate single-family homes; higher density development of flats was apparently envisaged. Even where land is available for construction of single-family units, the cost of infrastructure provision is often too high to be affordable to the household. Instead, households build under the threat of demolition, using old or recycled materials to keep costs down and limit their potential losses. This is a competitive solution to the housing shortage, but a very tenuous one.

Housing Allocation and Tenure

Housing in Yugoslavia is obtained primarily in one of two ways: (1) by being granted tenancy rights for a socially owned dwelling; or (2) by purchasing or constructing a unit with private funds, or with a combination of private and public funds. There is also a private rental market, but its development has been limited by the strong rights granted to tenants in Yugoslav law.

Allotment of social rental housing (i.e., housing developed by the state or SOEs)--which is highly desirable because of the low rents charged--is carried out through local housing authorities and SOEs. The availability of vacant units is advertised and applicants are selected on the basis of the relevant SOE regulations and laws of the particular republic or autonomous province. Need is one factor that influences a household's likelihood of gaining access to a social unit, but the position and function of household members in the SOE have an effect, too; higher qualifications and position tend to exert a positive influence on housing allocation. Also, because SOEs finance the construction of social housing for their workers (see note 6, below), the availability of units is higher in work organizations that have higher profits. In general, workers in the construction, mining, and health care industries have the least favorable access to housing. The 1981 census also indicated that workers with the highest skill or education levels tended to have greater access to social housing than workers in general.

Once a household has obtained access to a social rental unit, tenancy rights are very strong--they are described in the 1974 Constitution as "permanent and guaranteed"--and include inheritance rights and freedom from eviction. Thus, flats originally granted to needy households can be passed on to following generations irrespective of their need or socio-economic standing. Indeed, these tenancy rights (which practically preclude removal of the tenant under any circumstances) act as a significant block to the development of a private rental sector.

Even so, several factors should promote the development of a private rental sector: abolition of limits on the private ownership of rental units; strong demand from households unable to obtain social housing or afford to purchase their own unit; market rents (about three times higher than rents in social housing) generally paid by tenants in private units and sub-tenants of privately owned and socially owned dwellings. Still, Simoneti (1990) notes that because households can acquire tenancy rights in privately owned units, it is possible for a tenant to occupy the unit nearly free of charge, leaving the owner without (legal) recourse.

There are apparently no limitations on private real estate transactions. Privately owned dwellings can be bought and sold outright for cash or inherited, or can be purchased with a combination of a downpayment and credit. Units built by SOEs are being sold, with the SOEs permitted to keep the proceeds and to use them for plant and equipment. In practice, the strong rights of tenants in social housing make them the only viable buyers. However, to the extent that the sale prices do not reflect the true market value of the units (which is, in itself, a difficult question to answer), such sales serve only to reinforce the current distribution of benefits, raising equity concerns on the part of those households who do not have access to social housing.

Housing Finance

RENTAL HOUSING

Social housing constructed for rental is financed out of the income and profits of SOEs within a local district (commune) and through contributions by employees to housing construction funds. Housing communities act as the coordinating housing agency for local state enterprises and are responsible for carrying out the construction and maintenance of social housing. As stipulated in law, a portion of all SOEs' incomes (i.e., an earmarked tax) is used by the housing communities to build "solidarity" housing for the socially disadvantaged and workers in SOEs with low earning capacity. Housing built by the housing community specifically for SOE employees is funded through the SOE's joint consumption fund (i.e., an allocation out of net profits).[6] This source of funds provides the bulk of financing for social housing--72 percent of the total in 1986. Employees contributions to housing construction funds are only a marginal source of financing, accounting for less than 1 percent of funds in 1986.

These housing construction funds are normally held as deposits in a state bank and do not earn interest. The funds are then lent to work organizations to finance housing construction--in the past at interest rates of 4 to 10 percent and terms of 15 to 25 years. To qualify for a loan, the SOEs are also required to have deposits with the bank equal to 30 to 50 percent of the value of the loan.

The revalorization of credit in 1987 (to adjust the real value of loans which had been greatly eroded by inflation) resulted in much higher interest rates. (About 90 percent of all housing credit outstanding in 1986 was in the form of fixed-rate loans.) However, not all loans were subject to revalorization. Those that escaped adjustment have seen the real costs of their borrowings fall as inflation has continued.

Rents from existing social housing are supposed to provide another source of funds for housing construction. Traditionally, rents for social housing were to be set in a manner which provided for full amortization of the social housing stock during its lifetime. As a further step, rents were to be set even higher in order to remove the burden of financing social housing (except for solidarity housing, which was seen as a legitimate expense to be borne by the state and SOEs) out of SOE profits. Rents were initially set at 2 percent of housing unit value in 1960. This was to cover the operating costs and amortization of the existing social housing stock. The 1965 housing reform prescribed annual rents for social housing equal to 4 percent of the dwelling value, with half the rent proceeds earmarked for expanded production of social housing.

In practice, rent increases to attain this target have been substantially slowed or stalled since 1968. In the meantime, the growth of retail prices and wages has greatly outstripped increases in rents. For example, retail prices increased over twice as fast as rents during the period from 1980 to 1986. Under the 4-percent formula, an average two-room dwelling with a floor area of 54 square meters should have a monthly rent of YuD27,600 ($72.80 at the average 1986 official exchange rate) per month in 1986. The actual rent for such a unit in 1986 was only about a fifth of the mandated rent level. In some regions, laws passed by the various republics and autonomous provinces have kept rents even lower. In Serbia, for example, the amortization lifetime of the social housing stock in 1984, based on prevailing rent levels, was calculated to be 650 years. At these levels, not only do rents fail to cover the amortization costs of the unit, but they may also fail to cover the maintenance costs as well.

In 1984, the Amortization Law brought about a large increases in rents, aiming to bring annual rents back above the 2 percent of value target established in 1960. However, initial gains have been eroded by subsequent inflation and an inability to raise rents in line with other prices. A survey in 1986 found that tenants in socially owned dwellings expend only 4.0 percent of their incomes on housing expenditures and only 2.3 percent of their incomes on rent. These are among the lowest shares of income devoted to housing in Eastern Europe.

With the high cost of credit and the failure of rental streams to develop as a viable source of funds to finance further construction of social housing, housing communities and SOEs have turned to the households themselves as a source of finance. In Slovenia, for example, households are required to pay up to 20 percent of the cost of the unit in return for the right of tenancy in a social dwelling. (The funds are eventually returned to the tenants if they fulfill the conditions of tenancy as set out by the housing community.)

FINANCE FOR HOME PURCHASE

Individuals can finance private homeownership by making downpayments and obtaining loans through their work organizations or their banks. A portion of housing construction funds are set aside for financing private ownership; this is viewed as a way to leverage private funds and increase the production of housing from a given pool in the housing construction fund.

Remittances from household members employed abroad are a major source of private funds for households financing home ownership. Between 1965 and 1989, Vilogorac et al. (1990) estimate that over 700,000 migrant workers sent between $30 and $35 billion in remittances back to households in Yugoslavia. Of this amount, more than 70 percent was invested in housing, although a portion was also spent on renovating and maintaining existing housing. Only about 4 percent of households which received remittances and undertook investment in housing also relied on housing loans to finance their investment.

Mortgage and housing loans are also provided by commercial banks and savings and loan organizations. Workers associations generally borrow from the commercial banks, which obtain funds from depositors including individuals, workers associations, and financial intermediaries (mainly other banks). However, lending by commercial banks to individual households to finance home owner-ship is much less common. Only about 1 percent of banks' total assets are accounted for by home mortgages (Vilogorac et al. 1990). The S&L institutions raise their funds through deposits and limit their housing and mort-gage lending to local clients.

Before the revalorization of credit in 1987, loans with interest rates of 1 to 10 percent and terms of 10 to 30 years were common. The size of loans for which households qualified was determined by the downpayment the house-hold could provide (up to 20 percent of the purchase price of the dwelling). As a result, households raising the larg-est downpayments--particularly those with members working abroad and providing remittances--received the largest loans. With the high inflation of the late 1980s, this system granted the largest implicit subsidies to households with the highest incomes. Revalorization has raised the cost of servicing mortgage debt; all new lending is now in-dexed. This change has put home purchasers at a relative disadvantage compared to tenancy right holders in social housing, who pay rents far below market levels.

Future Directions in Housing Reform

Yugoslavia has already taken some positive steps to intro-duce market forces into the housing sector by raising inter-est rates and removing constraints on the private owner-ship of flats. Raising rents is a high priority; this is viewed mainly as a measure to recover costs and to maintain dwellings, but is also seen as a prerequisite for any major privatization effort (since low rents reduce the incentives for tenants to buy their units and discourage private inves-tors from developing commercial rental properties).

Currently, rents and utility prices have been frozen as part of the latest stabilization program. Simoneti (1990), in a paper presented to a World Bank conference, argues that the country should use this opportunity to develop a comprehensive housing reform strategy to tackle the problems associated with: (1) raising rents and protecting low-income households from rent increases; (2) weakening tenancy rights (e.g., transforming tenancy rights into a contractual relationship between owners and renters, and eliminating certain means of eviction protection); (3) strengthening incentives to control production costs; (4) raising and lending housing funds on a competitive basis; and (5) developing a more sophisticated property tax system.

Notes, chapter 7

1. The effect of subsidies on migration is discussed in Popovic (1988).

2. Unless otherwise indicated economic data are from EIU (1989d).

3. Except where otherwise noted, this data in this section is drawn from Popovic (1988) and Jeerkic et al. (1988).

4. Cooperatives play only a small role in total housing production.

5. Unlike elsewhere in Eastern Europe, almost all socialized housing is controlled and funded by SOEs. (See the section on housing finance for rental housing below for a more detailed explanation.)

6. The joint consumption fund may also be used to provide low-cost loans for housing purchase or construction by SOE employees (see below).

Chapter Eight

THE HOUSING SECTOR IN BULGARIA

Bulgaria's economic development over the past 40 years has been notable among Eastern European CPEs in that some productive specialization has been achieved in areas where the country has some comparative advantage rather than the typical approach of simply pushing forward with heavy industry. Since the mid-1970s, however, economic progress has been slow and problems have been accumulating. As in other CPEs, the economy has grown rigid and unresponsive; quality has remained low; initiative has been stifled.

The response to these problems has also been similar to that of other CPEs, although the Bulgarians (with the Romanians) have been the most cautious in their approach to reform. Ownership still remains almost entirely in the hands of the state and past attempts at reform have been hampered by frequent reorganization of economic structures and failure to provide adequate incentives to enterprise managers. Since the mid-1980s, there have been some significant economic reforms grouped under the umbrella of the New Economic Mechanism (NEM). These and the most recent liberalizations are discussed in detail below.

DEMOGRAPHIC TRENDS

Bulgaria's population has been growing slowly, increasing at a rate of only 0.3 percent between in the 1980s. In 1985 Bulgaria's population was 8.9 million, with 13 percent of the total in Sofia, the largest city. Although it has been official policy to encourage population growth (through the granting of child allowances), changes in social behavior in fact led to a falling birth rate. As a result, the proportion of young persons in the economy has been declining (see table 8.1). This should act to ease some of the future demand on the housing sector. However, Bulgaria does face an increasing social burden in terms of a rising dependency ratio. Improved economic performance is thus important in order to meet the growing demand for health and social services which accompany an aging population.

Bulgaria has become increasingly urban. Urbanization increased from 24 percent in 1946 to 70 percent in 1990. In the five-year period from 1980 to 1985 the population of Sofia increased 4.9 percent compared to Bulgaria's overall increase of 0.8 percent.[1] To limit Sofia's growth, residence permits are required for residence in the city. Still, growth there has continued at a rapid pace.

OVERVIEW OF ECONOMIC REFORM[2]

The demand for economic reform in Bulgaria is not as clear as that demonstrated in Czechoslovakia, Hungary and Poland. As noted above, reform initiatives had already

Table 8.1   BULGARIA--POPULATION TRENDS 1970-2000

	1970	1980	1990	2000
Total population (millions)	8.5	8.7	9.2	9.5
Percent of total				
Age 14 and under	22.8	22.1	22.0	20.6
Age 15-64	67.6	66.0	65.3	64.2
Age 65 and over	9.6	11.9	12.7	15.1
Dependency ratio[a] (percent)	47.9	51.5	63.2	55.7
Urban population (percent)	52.3	62.5	70.3	75.9
Annual growth (percent)				
Total	0.8	0.3	0.4	0.3
Urban	3.4	2.0	1.5	53.2
Rural	-1.8	-2.2	-2.0	-1.8

Source: United Nations (1986).

a. The dependency ratio is the sum of the population under age 15 and age 65 and over divided by the population age 15-64 expressed as a percentage.

been planned under the NEM, but were bringing about change only slowly. The recent reelection of the communist party was certainly not a vote for a radical restructuring of the Bulgarian economy.

State Enterprises and the Private Sector

The main aim of the NEM was to reduce central control over the enterprises by restricting the number of targets that could be set by the central planners and by using financial criteria for decision-making. Enterprises were expected to be self-supporting and responsive to market demand. Other modest reforms included: pay incentives for workers, increased reliance on worker self-management in enterprises, and specialization in banks and financial enterprises.[3,4] However, as has been the case in other CPEs that have attempted similar modest reforms, there was little in the way of positive results.

The most recent version of the NEM is Decree 56, which came into effect in January 1989. All enterprises were to be put on a profit and loss accounting basis and to begin developing the rudiments of a capital market through share sales to employees and other investors (both domestic and foreign). The national plan was no longer binding on enterprises and the 1989 plan contained few hard quantitative targets. Individuals were also given the right to start their own firms.

However, the principle of central control still remained entrenched. The Ministry of Economic and Planning can still issue a binding production order to any state enterprise at any time. The Ministry also controls the granting of state subsidies to cover losses, tax rates, rights to retain foreign currency, and many other key powers which give it substantial leverage over enterprise actions.

The government has now indicated a commitment to move toward free markets, but specific details remain vague. An illustration is offered by Glavanakov (1990), a government paper on future directions for reform. The paper emphasizes four objectives: (1) free markets, (2) competition, (3) decentralization, and (4) financial, monetary and interest rate reform. However, it gives no details on probable policies and programs. The country is discussing reform measures used earlier or considered by other Eastern European countries. For example, Bulgaria plans to hold limited auctions for currency and to tax firms that increase wages in excess of a cap. It also plans to set up a "safety net" for workers who lose their jobs, offering benefits and establishing centers to provide assistance to dislocated workers (as has been done in Poland and is planned in Hungary).

Recent reforms permit the ownership of private real property without restrictions. Bulgaria had permitted private ownership of *personal* property--including homes and small shops--prior to 1990 reforms. But Bulgaria has not dealt with the matter of transferring state property--housing and nonhousing--to the private sector.

Foreign ownership of critical property (for example, land, water rights, and minerals) is restricted. Foreign ownership in joint ventures (up to 49 percent) or leasing are the only means of providing foreign owners with access to the restricted properties.[5] Bulgarian firms were recently permitted to issue equity stock, but the procedure was envisioned to accommodate foreign rather than domestic investors.

Finance and Banking System

The Bulgaria banking system has been evolving toward a Western prototype, but with some important differences. In addition to its central bank, the Bulgarian National Bank, the country has seven large industry-related commercial banks--serving agriculture, chemicals, construction, engineering, electronics, infrastructure and transport--and a number of local banks recently established by dismantling part of the central bank. The commercial banks were established three years ago and these could provide a starting point for a capital market to allocate savings and credit to enterprise investments on the basis of highest expected returns.

Banks are socially owned but pyramid holding arrangements vest control in "owners"--large banks, particularly the central bank, and large enterprises. The commercial banks' directors, creditors, and borrowers overlap. Banks have also had little latitude in allocating funds; until recently, allocations still had to conform to centralized economic plans. However, banks are now to have more autonomy in client selection. How this will work out remains to be seen. But the commercial banks' specialized knowledge of particular industries runs the danger of generating loan portfolios that are not well diversified.

The central bank conducted central bank and investment bank functions until 1987. Economic reforms in the 1960s had attempted to separate the two functions but were subsequently reversed. Two special purpose banks serve foreign trade and innovative economic projects. The National Savings Bank provides most mortgage lending and also some commercial lending, but operates at a loss.

The current plan is for the central bank to regulate credit availability, interest rates and commercial bank operations. Commercial banks are to provide investment funds and monitor investment in enterprises. Recently the central bank was split from its 51 local district branches, each of which will operate autonomously in making a variety of business, home, and consumer loans. Whatever the loan mix, however, approximately 60 banks is far too many for Bulgaria, spreading scarce banking skills thin in a financial market which is still severely limited. Worse yet, the independent banks are not yet efficiently connected by financial intermediaries to ensure the efficient flow of financial resources from one to another.

Bulgaria's financial structure outside of the banking system is rudimentary. It has virtually no domestic bonds or stock-equity ownership, although reforms in this direction are a virtual certainty as the government has indicated that private and foreign ownership of enterprises would no longer be discouraged.

Prices

Controls apparently to have been lifted from about 40 percent of prices, but retained on crucial consumer goods (Galavanakov 1990). Inflation does not yet appear to be a serious problem. The 1990 forecast is for 10 percent (a more realistic assessment of price movements than past official statistics). Perry, Koleva and Popov (1990) estimate a rate of 15 percent and as much as another 10 percent annual inflation may be "hidden" by declines in quality and by "grey" markets. When controls are fully lifted, inflation will no doubt rise, since goods are in short supply and liquidity held by Bulgarians exceeds the country's total annual consumption expenditure.

THE HOUSING SECTOR

Like all Eastern European nations, Bulgaria faces housing shortages and difficulties in expanding production and improving productivity in the sector. These problems can be traced to reforms that crippled the private housing construction industry (active until restrictions were imposed in 1958) and the control over real estate and housing pricing granted to local government. The problems resulting from these policies are examined in greater detail below.

When measured as a share of national output and investment, the housing sector in Bulgaria is smaller than those in Poland and Hungary. In 1985, housing investment in Bulgaria amounted to 4.4 percent of NMP, about one-fifth lower than in Hungary (5.4 percent) and one-quarter lower than in Poland (6.1 percent). In terms of national investment, the differences are even more marked: housing in Bulgaria accounted for 12.8 percent of all investment in 1985, compared to 21.1 percent in Hungary and 24.6 percent in Poland. Evidence indicates the share of housing in national investment has remained static since 1985; the share of housing in national fixed assets has remained steady at 17.0 percent (United Nations 1988). The relatively low level of housing investment reflects the pressure on state construction companies to finish work on the large program of "productive" investments undertaken in the 1980s.

Housing accounts for about half the output of the construction sector--which made up 9.9 percent of national income in 1985 (EIU 1989e, United Nations 1989a). The building materials industry shows signs of low productivity, despite being one of the leading sectors for investment and promotion; output from the industry increased only at a rate of 1.3 percent annually during 1985-88.

Housing Stock and Production

The 1985 housing census counted a total of 3.1 million dwellings in Bulgaria, with 61 percent of the units located in urban areas.[6] Data on the average age of the stock is not available; approximately half the stock has been constructed since 1960. About 63 percent of the dwelling units are found in single- or two-family houses (although 83 percent of the new units built during 1981-85 were in multi-family buildings of three units or more). Ownership of housing in Bulgaria is predominantly private, with 84 percent of the housing stock owned by individual households. (In many rural villages, all housing is privately owned.) The remaining 16 percent is owned by municipal councils and state enterprises and forms the rental stock (Kolvea and Giorov 1990). Coverage of urban services in Bulgaria is high overall, with all settlements being electrified and water supplies available in 98.5 percent of all settlements. Virtually all new dwellings have bathrooms and hot water (Grigorov et al. 1987).

Housing production has been declining steadily since 1980, the number of new dwellings completed falling from 74,300 in 1980 to 63,000 in 1988. This level of production represents only 1.9 percent of the 1988 housing stock of 3.3 million units. Production in 1985, 64,900 units, amounted to only 80 percent of the number of new households formed, as measured by the total number of marriages and divorces (United Nations 1988). Parry et al. (1990) report that 330,000 households--representing about 15 percent of the country's population--are currently registered in the queue to buy or rent housing.

During 1980-84, 352,400 units of housing were produced, an average of 70,500 per year. In the following period, 1985-88, 247,600 units were produced. This implies a fall in the average annual rate of production of 12 percent, to 61,900 units per year. Since the share of housing in national output and investment has been broadly constant in the 1980s this fall implies declining productivity and rising unit costs in the sector. A shortage of manpower in the construction sector has contributed to the problem.

As gloomy as these overall production figures may be, the actual housing situation is worse. These global measures understate the extent of the housing shortage, since they do not take into account the mismatch between housing demand in urban areas (which has grown rapidly since the 1950s) and rural areas (which now have empty units).[7] In 1986, for example, the waiting list for housing in Sofia numbered 80,000 households, about 30 percent of the city's 1.1 million residents (Miskiewicz 1986). Currently, there is a 15-year waiting list to buy or rent housing in Sofia and a 10-year wait in most other large cities. In rural areas, large numbers of dwellings stand empty or have been acquired by city residents as vacation homes (Parry et al. 1990).

By some quality measures, the housing situation has improved since 1980; per capita floor space increased from 14.5 square meters (158 square feet) to 18.9 square meters (206 square feet) per person in 1988.[8] As of 1988, the average dwelling had 2.5 rooms and 51.1 square meters of floor space (United Nations 1989a). Newer units are being built larger; the average floor space for units constructed in 1985 was 57.7 square meters (Grigorov et al. 1987). However, there remain numerous complaints about the quality of planning, design, and construction of new housing.

Construction and Building Materials Industry

Because of the pressure of the housing shortage and the declining ability of the state sector to meet demand, recent actions have been taken to shift the burden of housing provision away from the state. This is a reversal of the policies of state centralization of housing construction in the late 1950s.

In 1958, the entire construction industry was nationalized and placed in the hands of a centrally directed national construction enterprise. At the same time, municipal councils were given responsibility for controlling housing construction. This new structure aimed to replace a diversified construction industry, which included private contractors, cooperatives, and self-help construction as well as numerous small SOEs. Private construction was squeezed out not only by restrictive regulations, but also by differential pricing of building materials. Materials provided to SOEs were subsidized. As a result, the share of private construction in housing production fell dramatically, from 53 percent in 1961 to 13 percent in 1976 (Parry et al. 1990).

In 1987, there were 88 SOEs in the construction sector, employing 266,000 workers (6.5 percent of the national work force). These enterprises tend to be large; 74 have work forces of more than a thousand employees (United Nations 1989a).

The restructuring of the construction industry coincided with the rapid growth of the urban population. The need to produce large numbers of housing units led the state sector to move away from traditional Bulgarian housing (single-family detached houses and low-rise town houses) and, following the path of other East European socialist economies, to concentrate on industrialized production of mid- and high-rise apartment buildings (although the emphasis on construction has lately been shifted from high- to low-rise construction).

This industrial method of building has caused problems in several cases where the local planning authorities have failed to provide adequately sized sites to accommodate the large-scale equipment needed to erect these blocks. As in other CPEs, SOEs in Bulgaria have been plagued with problems of low labor productivity, energy inefficiency (with respect to both production and performance of the finished units), and low and inconsistent quality of completed units. Efforts have been made to raise quality standards for state-produced housing units by involving new apartment owners in the finishing work for the units.

The switch to industrialized production greatly increased the average construction time for housing. This increase was the result not only of inefficiencies associated with centralized control, but also of abandoning traditional wood-frame methods--which could produce a dwelling in less than four months, compared to a year or more with industrialized processes.

Since 1981, when it produced 80 percent of all new dwellings, the state's share in housing production (including those built by the state for cooperatives) has been falling; still, the state produced 67 percent of housing built in 1988 (United Nations 1989a). To maintain overall production levels, other forms of state production, cooperatives, and private construction have received greater encouragement. Since 1983, state enterprises have been instructed to provide housing for their own workers, using their own resources and work force. Cooperatives, private construction by independent (i.e., "second" economy) contractors, and self-help housing have been allowed to produce housing in Bulgaria without interference as long as the housing is for personal use (McIntyre 1988). In 1988, 47 percent of all new housing was sponsored by the state sector (both local authorities and state enterprises building for their employees), 20 percent by cooperatives, with the remainder (33 percent) by the private sector (United Nations 1989a).

Official measures of private construction output (by value) do not reconcile with reported production levels. For example, according to government statistics, construction carried out by cooperatives, workers' associations, and private organizations accounted for only 6.6 percent of construction output in 1985 (Grigorov et al. 1987), yet cooperative and private investors produced 54 percent of all units completed that year (United Nations 1989a). Thus, the bulk of private construction activity is confined to the second economy outside the control of the central planning mechanism or takes the form of household self-help. This does not imply that this private activity is small in scale. For example, private construction and renovation of second houses for year-round and summer use (known as *dachas*) is widespread and dominated (particularly in rural areas) by three-storey houses of large size and good quality (McIntyre 1988).

Housing Allocation and Tenure

Until April 1990 all aspects of the pricing and transfer of real estate and housing were controlled by municipal governments in Bulgaria. This control meant that owners of housing units did not often wish to give up their current dwelling when they acquired another, and would maintain ownership of the original unit (legally or illegally) if at all possible. In April 1990 all constraints that had previously governed private housing transactions were lifted. Households are now able to exercise a full range of rights over housing and property, including setting prices and sale terms without intervention by local governments (Kolvea and Giorov, 1990). As yet, there still remains little readily available information on sale prices, forcing households to do their own research to discover price levels in the market.

State-sponsored housing is usually built by local authorities, some for rental but most for sale to owner-occupiers. If a household wishes to rent or buy a new or existing house, it must contact the local municipality, which determines the household's socio-economic suitability for being placed in the housing queue. When housing becomes available, it is allocated to the household at the top of the queue, at a price fixed by the municipal council.

The ranking system for the housing queue is based on age, number of children, income, the type of unit desired, and previous waiting time.

Municipalities not only develop housing on state-owned land, but have the right to expropriate privately held land for development. If the land is used for state housing, the municipality must compensate the private owners (and their adult children, if in need of housing) by giving them first priority to the new units. The owners of expropriated properties are required to pay the difference between the price paid for the land and the cost of the new housing unit offered. However, the municipal council may choose to waive this requirement in whole or part on the basis of the household's socio-economic status.

If a household wishes to undertake the construction of its own housing unit, it is required to follow a procedure similar to that for purchasing existing housing. When a suitable building lot is located, an application is made to the municipal council for permission to purchase the land (whether it is public or private land) and construct a housing unit. When this permission is received, households undertaking their own construction will face costs about twice as high as for state-sponsored construction because of the high cost of building materials and tradesmen working (illegally) in the second economy.

Prices for land are based on a tariff established by the Bulgarian government in 1973 and unchanged through 1987.[9] In 1987, the price of land for housing spanned a wide range. Such land cost from Lv1 to Lv6 ($1.16 to $6.95) per square meter in towns with populations of less than 100,000 versus Lv4 to Lv10 ($4.63 to $11.59) per square meter in cities with more than 100,000 residents.[10] In addition to the cost of land purchase, prospective home-builders must also pay for the right to construct a housing unit on the site. In 1987, this right was priced between Lv5 and Lv21 ($5.79 to $24.33) per square meter of built-up area in towns under 100,000 and between Lv8 and Lv27 ($4.27 to $27.31) per square meter of built-up area in cities of more than 100,000 inhabitants. Beyond these costs, which apply to all land sales, land purchasers may also face punitive taxes--up to Lv400,000 ($463,500) per hectare--if agriculturally useful land is converted to residential use (Grigorov et al. 1987).

Housing Finance

RENTAL HOUSING

Flats constructed by the municipal councils are usually financed by loans from the National Savings Bank. These loans carry an annual interest rate of 4 percent. (Although official inflation has been less than 3.5 percent annually since 1985, recent published reports in Bulgaria (EIU 1990d) now estimate that retail price inflation actually exceeded 10 percent annually during this period--implying negative real interest costs for mortgage borrowing.) If the housing is sold to households, the loan is paid off with the proceeds of the sale. If the housing is for rent, the cost of the interest on the loan (usually with a term of 30 years) and other repayment shortfalls are met out of the state budget.

Rents have not changed since 1967 and are insufficient to cover construction and maintenance costs (Parry et al. 1990). Local councils may increase the official base rent of Lv0.19 per square meter of usable floor space by as much as 27 percent, or lower it by as much as 50 percent, depending on unit characteristics. Therefore, a household with average annual net family income of Lv3,870 (1985 prices), and occupying a unit with 58 square meters of usable space, would pay a base rent equal to about 3.4 percent of its net income. The average amount spent on all housing costs (including rent and utilities) is about 11 percent of net household income (Grigorov et al. 1987). The low rents associated with state-owned apartments have also meant that the quality of service provision and upkeep in state housing has been poor. Maintenance and modernization work has not been carried out, and in several cities the water supplies and heating facilities in state housing are inadequate.

Owners of private dwellings may also rent their premises, but prices for these rentals are also controlled by the municipal council. Private rents are not permitted to exceed Lv2.00 per square meter and all private rental contracts are required to be registered with the municipal authorities. Because of these restrictions and the desire to keep housing available for children or other family members, households who control more than one housing unit often choose to leave their second unit vacant rather than rent it to tenants. Parry et al. (1990) report that the number of vacant units is increasing, not only in rural areas (where declining population makes this inevitable) but also in urban areas (which are characterized by large housing deficits).

FINANCE FOR HOME PURCHASE

With little volume in the private real estate market, there are no data available on free market prices for housing in Bulgaria. In the state-sponsored market, as noted above, prices are controlled by municipal governments, with large subsidies built into both the pricing and financing of home purchase.

In 1980, McIntyre (1988) reports, state-produced apartments built for cooperatives sold for between Lv10,000 and Lv20,000 ($11,600 and $23,200); household incomes at the time averaged Lv6,000 ($7,000). During 1979-88, housing prices increased by 12 percent, while construction costs increased by 36 percent. The widening difference between the sale price and construction costs has been met by subsidies from the central government budget. In 1988, these subsidies totalled Lv42 million, just over 0.1 percent of GDP.

Finance for housing purchase (at low, subsidized prices) has been available from the state at low interest rates and for long terms--a typical mortgage is for 70 percent financing, at 2 percent fixed rate of interest, over 30 years. With past inflation now estimated at about 11 percent annually during 1985-89 and current inflation running at 15 percent annually (EIU 1990d), these low interest rates confer large implicit subsidies on their recipients.

According to Parry et al. (1990), The National Savings Bank has been the main source of residential lending, with an annual loan volume of only about Lv350 million ($140 million). The Bank pays 1 percent on deposits, but offers a special account for accumulating a downpayment that pays 2 percent.[11] The Bank operates at a loss and is subsidized by central government revenues.

To qualify for any mortgage loan, the borrower need only meet two conditions: (1) permission from the municipal council to purchase the dwelling; and (2) mortgage payments that do not exceed 50 percent of income. (Other housing expenses, property taxes, and utilities are subsidized and account for only a small proportion of household income.)

Other programs offer even more favorable terms to borrowers who cannot qualify for the standard mortgage.

For example, households in the queue who obtain the right to purchase a unit but have insufficient savings for the downpayment, can obtain a 40-year loan of up to Lv25,000 ($10,000) with an annual interest rate of 2 percent and no downpayment. Another program makes 30-year loans at 2 percent annual interest rates (coupled with 5-year loans to cover the downpayment if the household does not have adequate capital) to current renters of housing owned by municipal councils.

Kolvea and Giorov (1990) report that two new banks are being established: a private bank with initial capitol of Lv10 million ($4.0 million) and a new savings bank with initial capitol of Lv2.5 million ($1.0 million). Both of these banks are expected to participate in mortgage finance.

Future Directions in Housing Reform

Bulgaria is moving forward with reforms very slowly, compared to the pace being followed in Poland and Hungary. Controls on the price of housing are being lifted, as are other restrictions on the sale of housing. A proposal to modify the Property Law was passed in the National Assembly in March 1990. Bulgarian citizens now have the right to possess real estate properties without restriction on their number, total floor space, location, or other characteristics.

The reforms will permit the sale of housing units at market prices and reduce the involvement of local councils in sales. Under the reformed system, the National Savings Bank is likely to remain as the primary source of housing finance. However, interest rates will probably be raised to market rates, with lenders charging the equivalent of the rediscount rate plus a fee for administrative costs and losses.[12]

Notes, chapter 8

1. Unless otherwise indicated economic data are from EIU (1989e and 1990d).

2. See Ganev (1989) for a discussion of the Bulgarian population's changing spatial distribution.

3. Self-management is examined in Petkov and Thirkell (1988). A conceptual treatment is offered by Walliamann and Stojanov (1989).

4. Information on the amount of pay incentives is provided by Debroy (1984). The share of earnings was stable in the period 1960 to 1980 at approximately 65 percent of total income. Bonuses constituted 11.8 percent of earnings in 1980, a decline from 1975. In the period 1960 to 1980 the minimum wage was roughly 50 to 60 percent of the average wage.

5. Decree 56, adopted in 1989, opened the door for foreign investment; however, marginal tax rates were prohibitive. The tax rates were lowered in 1990 but indicate the sort of administrative complexity Bulgaria must confront to make foreign investment more attractive.

6. Data in this paragraph is from Grigorov et al. (1987).

7. During 1950-85, the urban population of Bulgaria grew at an average rate of 4.0 percent annually. Rural population, in the same period, declined by an average of 1.9 percent per year (United Nations 1986).

8. Floor space is defined here as the floor area of habitable rooms and does not include bathrooms, toilets, corridors, kitchenettes, or outdoor porches or balconies.

9. It is unclear if the April 1990 land price return also applies to state-owned land or if the official pricing schedule remains in effect.

10. US dollar equivalents are calculated based on the official exchange rate.

11. The National Savings Bank also offers several special loan packages to assist with the downpayment problems of younger households.

12. According to Parry, Koleva, and Popov (1990), the Banking Laws were recently changed to permit the creation of nine new commercial banks. While there is some discussion that these banks will become privately owned, they are presently government controlled. Decree 56, passed in January 1989, contains language permitting wider privatization efforts.

Chapter Nine

THE HOUSING SECTOR IN ROMANIA

Two features are dominant in Romania's development. The first is a history of high industrial growth, achieved not through greater efficiency and innovation, but by maintaining high levels of input growth: capital, labor, and raw materials. With slowing population growth and bottlenecks in domestic input supplies (such as energy and raw materials), strains began to appear in the economy beginning in 1977. Although official figures indicate that output growth has recovered since 1983, many Western observers treat the statistics with suspicion and believe output has continued to stagnate through the 1980s (EIU 1989f).

The second dominant feature of the Romanian economy has been the successful drive to eliminate the country's foreign debt. The country was relatively debt-free in 1990, but at the cost of vital imports of energy, raw materials, and capital goods. The result has been a massive decline in the competitiveness of Romanian industry. It has been forced to work with outmoded technology (many industries are still using technologies dating from the 1940s), and endemic shortages of many basic consumer goods, pushing Romania's standard of living down to one of the lowest levels in Europe.

Romania faces the greatest challenge of all the Eastern European countries surveyed in this report, in attempting to overcome the economic problems associated with its socialist past. Its economy had been the most rigidly controlled and its population and new government seem the least enthusiastic about moving toward a market economy. They are explicitly aiming toward a mixed economy that retains a strong state sector (with decentralized investment planning) joined with a revived private sector (reinforced by joint ventures with foreign investors). It remains to be seen if Romania can gain the benefits of market dynamism and efficiency while holding on to the stability of state control.

DEMOGRAPHIC TRENDS

Romania's population is 23.8 million. Population growth has been steadily slowing over the past 30 years and appears to be stabilizing at 0.7 percent annually in the 1990s (see table 9.1). The low population growth rate is due partly to a decline in the birth rate (from 20 per thousand in 1975 to 14 per thousand in 1983), and partly to a slight increase in the death rate over the same period. The change in both rates may simply be due to lower living standards, part of the legacy of neglected investment in social infrastructure resulting from the country's programs of industrial growth and debt repayment. Under the Ceausescu government, Romania had a pronatal policy, imposing extra taxes on single persons and childless couples.

Romania is one of the least urbanized countries in Europe, with just over half its population living in urban areas. The pattern of settlement was almost transformed by the policy of "systematization" of rural villages. This program, initiated in April 1988, would have eliminated

Table 9.1   ROMANIA--POPULATION TRENDS 1970-2000

	1970	1980	1990	2000
Total population (millions)	20.4	22.2	23.8	25.5
Percent of total				
Age 14 and under	25.9	26.7	24.4	23.7
Age 15-64	65.5	63.1	65.3	64.2
Age 65 and over	8.6	10.3	10.2	12.5
Dependency ratio[a] (percent)	52.6	58.6	53.0	55.9
Urban population (percent)	41.8	48.1	50.4	53.2
Annual growth (percent)				
Total	1.4	0.9	0.7	0.7
Urban	3.4	1.7	1.2	1.3
Rural	-0.1	0.1	0.1	0.1

Source: United Nations (1986).

a. The dependency ratio is the sum of the population under age 15 and age 65 and over divided by the population age 15-64 expressed as a percentage.

7,000 of Romania's 12,000 rural villages and replaced them with 600 urban centers with factories, services, and blocks of flats (Hunya 1989). This policy was one of the first to be cancelled by the reform government that took control at the end of 1989. Cancellation of the program, which was beginning to be implemented in earnest, averted an economic catastrophe. Not only was the program enormously disruptive in social terms, but it was also absorbing about *half* the total capacity of the construction sector and diverting resources to replace existing serviceable housing rather than providing additional new housing in areas of shortage.

OVERVIEW OF ECONOMIC REFORMS[1]

In 1990, Romania has approached economic reform in a hesitant manner. First, the country had few experiments in economic reform; tightly controlled central planning prevailed. Second, the new government stated from the outset that the reforms would take at least five years to carry out, and that its aim was for an economic structure that allowed private control of agriculture and small business but left both heavy and light industry under mainly nationalized ownership. There was an initial burst of activity to relieve the most onerous aspects of the Ceausescu government's economic system but further reform has proceeded more slowly, making Romania the least advanced Eastern European CPE in its reform efforts.

State Enterprises and the Private Sector

The industrial sector is still almost entirely in the state's hands and accounts for over 40 percent of the labor force of 11 million. This alone is forcing the government to move slowly on reform. Politics also plays a part. The 1990 election confirmed that protection of employment and stability are still seen as more valuable than the gains from a Polish-style shock treatment.

SOEs play a key role in the Romanian economy over and above their domination of the industrial sector. Over 95 percent of Romanian government revenues come from taxes paid by enterprises. Taxes on individuals were reduced steadily through the 1980s, although about 15 percent of revenues were raised from taxes levied on SOE wage funds. The SOEs also provide many of the social services--health, education, housing, and pensions, for example. Displacing the SOEs from this leading role could cause both economic and social disruptions even larger than those experienced in Poland.

Although reform of the SOEs has not yet begun, efforts are underway to start lifting the constraints on the private sector. Private ownership of homes and family businesses has been allowed under the new reforms and the government has announced that the scope of private ownership would be expanded. Private businesses, on a limited basis, were legalized. Establishments with less than 20 employees are now allowed (with the limit soon to be raised to 100); by June 1990 over 30,000 applications had been registered for opening new private businesses (East European Markets, 1990). Plans also call for free market prices in the private enterprise sector. In addition, some state employees are to be allowed to work part-time in private businesses.

Romania was one of the first East European CPEs to allow joint ventures with equity participation by foreign investors. The legislation, passed in 1971, met with little success, however. More restrictive than current Polish and Hungarian regulations on joint ventures, the Romanian rules restricted foreign participation to 49 percent, limited the repatriation of hard currency profits, and taxed those profits at discriminatory rates. These restrictions, operating problems, and Romania's economic problems in the 1980s have so far deterred Western investors.

Prices and Wages

Before the reforms of 1990, Romanian prices provided unusually poor market signals, since most goods were unavailable or only offered with restrictions. For example, electricity was available to residences only a few hours a day and at very high rates under the Ceausescu government until 1990. The new government has moved to lift the supply restrictions. Households now receive twice the share of electric power produced compared to 1989, and many foods and consumer goods not seen for years have reappeared in shops. Unlike other reforming CPEs, however, Romania has not yet moved to lift controls on prices (although some prices are being selectively reduced), fearful of the instability which free prices could bring to the country.

Inflation in excess of 10 percent is expected for 1990. Observers think this is probably not far out of line from recent experience although official inflation data has not been reported since the mid-1980s. The Romanian Labor Minister, for example, has said that wages levels will be maintained, despite wide acknowledgment that production is falling and will continue to fall through the first stages of economic restructuring.

Financial and Banking System

Romania's financial system is primitive but follows the standard model in centrally planned economies. Romania has a two-tier banking system; (1) the Romanian State Bank (central bank) and (2) specialized banks. The central bank's guiding policy has been to prevent inflation by equating disposable income with the value of consumer goods. The specialized Romanian banks provide credit on a pass-through basis from the central bank to the borrowing client.

The Romanian central bank has local branches, but both its branches and the specialized banks are virtually arms of the public treasury. The banks direct funds to accommodate client plans; the client plans provide the instructions for a command economy. The branch banks simply compare firm requests to firm plans and monitor implementation. Hence, there is no loan underwriting as it is understood in the West, where banks evaluate the riskiness of loans and ability of borrowers to service the loan.

Specialized banks include the Investment Bank, the Agricultural Bank, the Foreign Trade Bank and the Savings and Deposit Bank. The Savings and Deposit Bank (and its branches) receive deposits from individuals and municipalities, siphoning off liquidity. The Savings Bank lends the deposits to the State Bank (central bank). The State Bank typically has used the funds for housing loans. The Investment and Agricultural Banks distribute investment funds according to the central plan.

Interest rates are set arbitrarily by the Central Bank. In recent years rates have been raised; however, rate setting has not been used to allocate investment. Recently some consideration has been given to allowing enterprises to issue equity shares or bonds, but these financial instruments are not currently available. Romania has no financial market and virtually no institutions other than the structural "shells" provided by the banks.

The currency, the leu, is not convertible. Romania has announced no plan or intention to move toward convertibility, so the country's economy is likely to remain isolated. The economy continues to be centrally planned with little market orientation. This is not surprising since reforms so far are designed more to fill in gaps left in the socialist economy than to make basic structural changes.

THE HOUSING SECTOR

Housing Production and Delivery

Romania has the smallest proportion of its national income devoted to the housing sector of any East European country. In 1985, housing investment in Romania amounted to 2.3 percent of NMP, less than half the share in Poland and Hungary; 6.1 percent and 5.4 percent, respectively (United Nations 1988). The only other country in the region with a similarly low proportion was the German Democratic Republic, but in 1985 East Germany showed production levels per capita almost three times as high as in Romania.

In terms of national investment, Romania again is the lowest in Eastern Europe, devoting only 8.1 percent of total investment to housing in 1985. All other countries in the region devoted more than 12 percent of their total investment to housing in that year--and Poland and Hungary devoted more than 20 percent. Productivity in Romania's housing sector has also fallen. The number of units constructed fell by 47 percent between 1980 and 1985 while the volume of resources devoted to housing decreased by only 37 percent in real terms (United Nations 1988).

Housing in Romania has always been central to Romanian social policy, in terms of both resolving persistent housing shortages and achieving the state's desired pattern of urbanization. Under the Ceausescu regime, as noted, the country undertook massive programs of reconstruction and consolidation of cities, towns, and villages. In urban areas the key components of these plans were the clearing of city centers of their historic buildings and replacing them with new street networks and large blocks of commercial and residential buildings. In rural areas, the plans called for relocation of hundreds of thousands of persons (cutting the number of rural villages from 13,000 to about 6,000) and replacing existing rural housing with blocks of flats (Hunya 1989). These programs have been stopped by the new administration.

These programs explain the large urban bias in new housing construction. During 1976-80, in sharp contrast, of the 841,800 new housing units built, nearly 90 percent were built in rural areas--despite the fact that just under half the population lived in rural areas (Miskiewicz 1986).

Housing production has been unable to keep up with household formation; the number of new units produced in 1985 represented only 54 percent of the number of new households created by marriage and divorce that year (United Nations 1988). And this global measure understates the housing shortage, since it takes account neither of the number of units lost from the housing stock due to clearing sites in city centers and consolidation of rural settlements, nor of household dissatisfaction with the quality of present housing.

For example, in Bucharest, the waiting list for new housing numbers over 100,000 applications, which could represent as much as 15 percent of the city's 2.3 million residents. Most of these applications represent households seeking better quarters (Nankman 1990). There are few options open to them. Contracting directly with SOEs to build dwelling units does not necessarily improve access to housing--private individuals who do so may have to wait as long as two to three years after the order is placed for the work to be carried out (Dorin 1990). Private construction of new housing is difficult because of the shortage of building sites and inadequate supply of building materials (Nankman 1990).

One strong indication of the housing shortage is the number of persons living in single workers' hostels: 561,000 in 1984. These hostels lack basic facilities, such as kitchens, but are often used even by young married households as no other shelter is available. Many residents have spent up to 10 years in a hostel waiting for a proper housing unit (Miskiewicz 1986). In addition to the hostels, significant numbers of workers live in other temporary shelters on construction sites and at forestry and oil-extraction operations.

Housing production in 1985 (106,000 units) was 47 percent lower than in 1980 (198,000 units). This downward trend in annual production partially explains the 16 percent fall in total housing production during the 1981 to 1985 period compared to the previous five years (United Nations 1988; Miskiewicz 1986).

Construction Industry

Housing in Romania is produced both by the socialized sector (which includes the state, SOEs, and cooperatives) and by private individuals. In 1980, the socialized sector accounted for 94 percent of all new housing; the private sector produced only 11,200 units that year (United Nations, 1988). These units were built almost exclusively in rural areas, as building individual units in urban areas was prohibited.

Housing built by the state over the past 40 years has conformed to a limited range of standardized flats in large blocks. At present they are built to three basic standards, with up to 5 habitable rooms, a kitchen, and 1-2 bathrooms. Floor space ranges from 24 square meters for a "low-comfort" one-room unit to 171 square meters for a five-room "increased-comfort" unit. Units with 3-4 rooms (ranging from 100 to 150 square meters) are most in demand. The production of flats with shared kitchen and bath facilities was stopped a few years ago and such units are now being renovated into larger and better-equipped flats (Nankman 1990).

Housing quality is a serious problem. Official statistics indicate that the amount of floor space per person increased from 31.9 square meters in 1970 to 35.2 square meters in 1980 (Miskiewicz 1986). However, the quality of construction has declined considerably over the past 15 years and that of new units is extremely poor, due to lack of skilled labor, inadequate supplies of materials and spare parts, and poor management of time and equipment. According to one observer (Gilberg 1990) the quality of construction and materials is so poor that many new blocks of flats are slums even before the scaffolding is taken down.

The private sector construction industry did not formally exist before 1989, when legislation allowing the creation of private enterprises was enacted. Most private activity is still carried out as it was previously: as small-scale, for workers with formal jobs in the state construction sector. Private sector construction costs are about 4,000 to 5,000 lei per square meter ($33 to $42 per square meter at the current mean unofficial exchange rate of 120 lei per dollar), significantly higher than reported public sector units costs of 3,000 lei per square meter (Nankman 1990). This price differential illustrates the different operating conditions that the two sectors face. The public sector cost probably reflects some scale economies, but also some hidden subsidies; the higher private sector costs are due to the higher prices paid for labor and material as well as the more speculative nature of the work.

Private construction is currently confined to private land; no public land, serviced or unserviced, is being made available for private development. And there is no sign of any near-term change in this policy, though the possibility of serviced, leasehold plots for individual construction by young families and first-time owners has been raised.

Housing Allocation and Tenure

The trend in housing tenure in Romania during 1948-89 has been towards greater restrictions on private control.

Nationalization of housing in 1948 restricted private ownership to one unit per household, with most other units confiscated and turned into public sector housing (Nankman 1990). It has been possible (in theory) since 1973 for private individuals to construct and purchase individual dwelling units (either from other individuals or from the state). However, as Dorin (1990) reports, the 1973 legislation was not followed by contractual and administrative procedures adequate for its implementation. As a result, further legislation to protect the rights of purchasers (mainly to give recourse against poor-quality construction produced by the SOEs) was promulgated in 1977. Even this measure did not lead to an appreciable increase in the number of flats and houses being built, as households found legal recourse difficult and usually ended up simply paying for the necessary repairs themselves. In practice, most private sector activity since the 1970s has focused on renovating existing privately owned buildings.

During the 1979 to 1985 period, tenants were able to buy, under very favorable terms, the rental flats which they occupied. Sales were suspended in 1985 as part of a generalized drive against private ownership, however. Under current law (as modified in 1990), these sales have been allowed again, with the intention of both absorbing excess liquidity in the economy and responding to popular demand for housing ownership. The proceeds from the sale of state-owned flats are transferred to the central government. However, the property rights associated with these sales are confused; the sites on which multi-family units sold to their occupants were constructed remain owned by the state, for example, but the units themselves are owned by their occupants. Although no figures are yet available, observers think that the lifting of restrictions against the sale of public and private dwellings in 1990 has revived the real estate market and brought about signs of significant activity (Nankman 1990).

Housing Finance

Rents on state-owned flats are determined by a formula that takes into account tenant income, household size, and floor area (but not location). Typical rents range from 100 to 1,000 lei per month ($4.55 to $45.50 at the present official exchange rate of 22 lei per dollar) and represent about 10 percent of household incomes (Nankman 1990). Dorin (1990) estimates that rents on state-owned flats are about half free-market rents. If so, this would be much closer to market levels than rents in other East European countries. Higher rents are plausible because of the Romanian legal standard of 10 square meters of housing per person; households living in units that exceed this standard pay significantly higher rents.

Finance for housing purchase during the 1979-85 period was provided through the Romanian Bank for Investments. Loans were structured according to salary and size of unit: downpayments increased from 20 percent to 30 percent and loan terms fell from 25 to 15 years as salaries rose; loan ceilings ranged from 35,000 lei ($2,300 at the 1981 official exchange rate) for a one-room flat to 90,000 lei ($6,000) for a five-room flat; and interest rates ranged from 3 percent to 8 percent according to the type of loan granted. It was also possible, in rural and some urban areas, for households to obtain a loan of 25,000 lei ($1,700) for building their own unit. In most urban areas, though, households could only qualify for a loan if they were buying an existing unit or one built by a SOE developer; no financing was available for individual construction (Dorin 1990).

In 1990, the restrictions on housing purchase were lifted and households were allowed to obtain credit from state banks to finance individual unit construction. Finance for housing purchase remains almost entirely in the hands of the state, however, with no increases in credit evident for the private housing sector. Current mortgage loans have terms of 20-25 years, and loan-to-value ratios of 70 percent and higher. Annual interest rates are between 2 and 6 percent, and the official inflation rate is under 2 percent annually. Prices are very low. In May 1990, for example, single family units with 300-400 square meters of floor space in the better locations in Bucharest were selling on the private market for between one and two million lei ($8,500 to $17,000 at the unofficial exchange rate). Vacant sites suitable for in-fill development in similar locations were selling for 1,200 lei ($10) per square meter. It is not yet known how deep this market might be, as the true scope of land and properties in private hands is only now being assessed.[2] In addition, most privately owned buildings are at least 20 years old (with the majority constructed about 40 years ago) and in varying states of disrepair.

Future Directions for Reform

No statement has yet been made on housing policy, but Nankman (1990) outlines the following probable features of future reforms in the Romanian housing sector:

- Continued strong state involvement, especially on the production side, but targeted more narrowly on the middle- and lower-income sections of the population. A countrywide program of 85,000 units to be built by local authorities has recently been approved. The units would mainly be 100 square meter rental units with monthly rents set at 400-500 lei. There would be purchase options at cost prices of 150,000 lei to 300,000 with conventional long-term, low-cost financing.

- No significant rental increases, either through raising public housing rents or relaxation of private rental controls.

- Enlarged scope for divestiture of existing public housing and sale of new units, by widening existing programs and offering purchase options for newly built public rental housing. A draft divestiture law proposes sale prices of 7,000 to 8,000 lei per square meter and a prohibition on resale for five to ten years. Privatization of the older state housing stock is clouded by claims of former owners (and their estates) on units previously nationalized.

- Greater--but as yet unspecified--scope for private sector activity. This is not a high government priority. The spurt of activity following the relaxation of restrictions on the private sector is likely to be short-lived rather than developing into a sustained private real estate market, unless action is taken quickly to remove the many handicaps that the private sector faces-- rent controls, subsidized price competition from the public sector shortages of serviced land, credit, and building materials.

Notes, chapter 9

1. Unless otherwise indicated economic data are from EIU (1989f, 1990e).

2. Apparently, the cadastral records are in good order and have been kept up to date.

Chapter Ten

TRANSITION ISSUES

The previous chapters have suggested a number of issues that the Eastern European economies will have to face in the process of reorienting their housing sectors so that production and allocation decisions are made by market forces rather than by government bureaucrats. This chapter integrates the previous points and systematically discusses transition issues. These issues fall into three interrelated groups: housing finance, housing development, and the state rental sector.

Perhaps the greatest challenge in reform is attempting to deal with all of these areas at the same time; while simultaneous action is not absolutely essential, we argue that it is difficult to avoid because of the extent to which finance, development, and rental issues are connected.

HOUSING FINANCE

The first step in developing an effective system of housing finance is to find ways to deal with the artificially cheap long-term debt that is the legacy of the past.

Dealing with the Past

In the 1980s several of the countries reviewed made low interest mortgage loans to households for home purchase. Often they were motivated to do so by the wish to avoid the large future subsidies associated with maintaining additional state rental units. Nevertheless, these fixed rate mortgage loans, at interest rates of 2 and 3 percent, now involve enormous subsidies, because as economic liberalization progresses, officially recognized inflation rises--as do the interest rates paid by lenders on deposits. The resulting large negative spread experienced by the state savings bank between earnings on mortgage assets and the cost of liabilities must be covered by the central bank through loans or, what is preferable from an economic management perspective, explicit budget expenditures.

Dealing explicitly with this problem has profound implications for the development of the banking sector generally. Recall that in the traditional centrally planned economy, the central bank and a few specialty banks (e.g., trade and agriculture) handled commercial banking, and a state savings bank was responsible for raising deposits and consumer banking. The savings bank did the mortgage lending and is now the institution with the mismatch of assets and liabilities. In order for the financial system to become more competitive during economic reforms the newly recreated commercial banks must compete with the savings bank for deposits. However, as long as the savings bank is saddled with the low yielding mortgages (without compensating payments from the central bank or government), it cannot raise its interest rates on deposits without hastening its collapse. The legacies of making cheap mortgage credit available are restricted competition in the financial sector, low deposit interest rates, and small incentives for households to hold their assets in financial form.

The Hungarian government took the brave step in 1989 of buying the block of low interest loans from the state savings bank (OTP) and paying prevailing interest on bonds it sold to finance them. Thus, this enormous subsidy is "on budget", as described in the final section of chapter 4. OTP can compete with commercial banks for deposits. Even now, however, government is hesitant to allow interest rates on deposits to rise, since its expenditures on its bonds are thereby increased; the result is deposit rates that are somewhat below market levels.

An urgent question is what can be done to increase the interest rates on these outstanding loans. Most of these have another 10-15 years or more before they mature and the borrowers have very little reason to want to prepay. In some countries, such as Poland, the mortgage contract permits a revision in interest rates. The Poles raised rates sharply in January 1990 when adjustable rate mortgages were introduced ex post, with the state absorbing a limited share of the higher payments. At this point, the extent to which defaults were induced is unclear; but the rapid decline in inflation (and interest rates) after the introduction of adjustable rate mortgages may have minimized this problem. In Hungary an attempt by government to raise rates was disallowed by the courts. The Hungarians are now thinking about defining the difference in mortgage payments between market levels and the 3 percent interest rates as a subsidy to be valued as income to the borrower that would be taxable under the country's new income tax. The progressive taxation of benefits would fit well with Hungarians sense of fairness. In any event, the stock of low interest rate mortgages is a major problem that cannot be ignored in restructuring the housing finance system in most Eastern European countries.[1]

Making New Mortgage Loans

The one principle on which nearly everyone agrees, especially in light of the disastrous "overhang" of past problems from cheap loans, is that market interest rates should be charged on new loans. Moreover, since a large part of the problem with the portfolio of outstanding loans results from the inability to adjust interest rates over time, adjustable rate mortgages (ARMs) are favored. Both Poland and Hungary have adopted ARMs, although it is not clear exactly how the indexing will work.

One should be careful, however, not to confuse the shift to market interest rates with ending subsidies. In many Eastern European countries the ratio of average house prices to average household incomes is 15-20 to 1. This compares with 3 to 1 in the United States and 8 to 1 in West Germany, which is considered high even by European standards. Under these conditions, and with higher interest rates (typically in double digits and sometimes over 20 percent because of inflation), households would have to postpone home purchase for many years while they save a large share of the purchase price. Obviously, there is tremendous pressure for government to "help" families become homeowners. When the Hungarian government went to market interest rates on mortgages, they also implemented an array of subsidies to keep homeownership affordable. While on balance the new subsidies are smaller than the old ones, they are still very large. Similar pressures--and responses--can be expected in other countries.

Economists at the World Bank and elsewhere are arguing that the affordability problem can be addressed at least partially through use of mortgage instruments better designed for the comparatively volatile and uncertain economic conditions that will characterize Eastern Europe over the next decade. Specifically, they argue that it is essential to shift to instruments that rearrange the mortgage payments in time. Instead of the fixed interest rate mortgage with high real payments in the early years, they should shift to instruments that keep real payments more constant over the life of the loan.

A particularly attractive instrument is the Dual Index Mortgage (DIM), under which a positive real interest rate is charged, and monthly payments are indexed to a wage rate index and the mortgage principal is indexed to a price index. Any divergence between the two indices results in adjustments to the loan's maturity; when some maximum maturity is reached (if inflation continually outstrips wages), monthly payments are increased. The price-level-adjusted mortgage is another instrument which spreads the burden of repayments more evenly over the term of the mortgage. The DIM, which is used in Mexico and is being seriously considered for adoption by several other countries, has the advantage of protecting the borrower from payment increases when wages in the overall economy are stagnant or falling; it then compensates by increasing payment more when wages accelerate.[2]

The central point is that housing affordability will be a major problem under a system in which full costs are charged for dwelling units and mortgage finance. Employing a mortgage instrument well suited for these circumstances can greatly mitigate (but certainly not eliminate) the affordability problem. Where some subsidy is still viewed by the state as being essential, it should be on budget and in the form of an up-front payment; as such its cost will be absolutely clear, as will the size of the benefit going to different households.

Construction Period Finance

Although SOEs constructing housing continue to have no trouble obtaining financing for developing housing, a clear pattern is that small firms have serious difficulty getting loans from commercial banks for the same purpose. The central problem appears to be the lack of underwriting skills on the part of loan officers at the commercial banks. When confronted with loan applications they cannot evaluate, and which are not SOE applications that are automatically approved, loan officers have every incentive to turn down the loan.

Obviously, there is a clear need for training to upgrade the underwriting skills of loan officers. While some general skills training in underwriting will probably be provided with assistance from the donor community (i.e., World Bank, EEC, and bilateral aid agencies) to the financial sector in each country, real estate loans are sufficiently different and complex that they will require special attention.

The need for skilled underwriting is likely to be increasingly important for two reasons. First, small firms will be accounting for a larger share of total production. If they have difficulty obtaining financing, production will lag and costs may increase. Second, if government wishes to impose a "hard budget constraint" on construction SOEs, the commercial banks will be key in implementing the constraint--and to do so they will have to be able to evaluate the proposals brought to them by the SOEs. Thus, construction period financing has a critical role to play in the transformation of the sector.

Relying on the Financial Sector

In some Eastern European countries SOEs have become active participants in financing housing. In Hungary, for example, the primitive nature of the banking system combined with high dwelling prices made it difficult for many households to finance home purchase; their employers have assisted with grants or cheap loans, some of the cost of which is a deductible business expense. In Yugoslavia, in contrast, SOEs' profits have been taxed to finance the development of new social housing--reflecting limitations of financial markets and the wish of government to avoid direct expenditures for housing development.

These arrangements are manifestly inefficient, since they generally involve organizations without expertise acting as bankers. At least as important, they often lack the incentives to conduct these transactions efficiently: since most SOEs have been subject to soft budget constraints, losses they might incur in giving overly generous grants or loans for housing are really absorbed by the banking system (and ultimately by the national budget). It is imperative to shift the burden of financing housing explicitly to the banking system and for all subsidies to be included in the state budget. Under the current system, national decision makers have little idea of the full subsidies involved in providing housing services and therefore they are in a weak position to make informed decisions about the need and direction of reform.

HOUSING DEVELOPMENT

There is general agreement that housing production by the SOEs has been remarkably inefficient and that productivity has deteriorated in the past decade. There is less appreciation of the fact that private contractors, too, are probably quite inefficient. Their potential efficiency is undermined by the difficulty (and cost) of assembling sites, raising financing (mostly equity participation), and locating materials. The materials are often produced by state enterprises in monopoly positions and are frequently of inferior quality, so that some must be replaced completely or adjusted on the work site.

The current extent of inefficiency has a bright side: the real price of housing production can be expected to fall, possibly considerably, over the medium term (perhaps five years), as competition produces improved quality in building materials and more efficient production practices and as the land management practices of local governments improve. Measuring this price decline will be difficult, however. As various subsidies are withdrawn--i.e., market rates are charged for sites and building materials--producers will face hard budget constraints that will cause them to raise prices. Thus, observed prices may well increase even though the price of completed dwellings, comprehensively measured, will probably decline.

Construction of Dwellings

Three groups are now producing housing in Eastern European countries: SOEs, small private contractors, and individual households.[3] The importance of each group varies sharply among countries. The SOEs are now least important in Hungary and most important in Czechoslovakia and Bulgaria, where they accounted for about 75 and 50 to 75 percent of production, respectively, as recently as 1987. There are rapid shifts among producers underway in Eastern Europe and in general it appears that the CPEs differ only in the speed of the shift toward self-help and private contractors.

The prior dominance of the huge SOEs is widely recognized, as is their low productivity. Consumers clearly also find their massive projects unappealing. Where consumers have been given a choice, the demand for SOE-produced units has plummeted. In Hungary, for example, several SOEs have already gone out of business and others are likely to follow over the next couple of years. How to deal with the remaining SOEs is an issue that cannot be ignored by government. On the one hand, addressing their future--particularly privatizing them--involves all of the ownership issues common to the future of SOEs generally in these economies.[4] On the other hand, the future demand for their product may be easier to forecast than for other types of SOEs since they produce wholly for the domestic market. The central question is whether they can be salvaged and made competitive by shedding some functions (such as materials production, in-house architectural services, and in-house staffing of various specialty construction occupations) and adopting more efficient production methods--especially taking advantage of subcontracting for a range of services. (In the United States, the typical general contractor subcontracts for three-fourths of the value of production on a multifamily project.)

A related question is whether SOE management can learn to respond to consumer preferences. In this regard, we are aware of at least one very large SOE in Budapest that has radically transformed the design of its new projects. In the past this firm developed for captive markets: state rental housing or units built for housing cooperatives, where all the units had already been sold. It is now building units on a speculative basis for sale to individual households. But it is clear that even this firm still receives very substantial preferential treatment from the local council in obtaining sites and from the commercial banks for construction period financing.

It remains to be seen whether the SOEs recast as private firms or continuing as profit-oriented state entities will be able to compete on a level playing field. Nevertheless, one should not assume that they will become extinct. As suggested, some at least have the leadership to try to adapt.

Private Contractors

Without question leveling the playing field between the SOEs and the emerging private contractors is the key issue for fostering the development of a competitive residential construction industry. Small private firms are clearly disadvantaged in obtaining financing, access to building materials and in some cases labor, assembling building sites, and being permitted to compete for state-commissioned projects.[5] Government action is needed in all of these areas to eliminate these impediments.

Beyond the availability of development period financing possibly the greatest obstacle in major urban areas is obtaining buildable sites. As discussed further in the next section, to date local governments are not carrying out their land development functions in a way that produces serviced land for small subdivisions. Moreover, the typical land zoning process makes it difficult for a private developer to get a parcel he might purchase from a private seller zoned for residential development. Private developers, therefore, concentrate on buying in-fill sites or building on sites that the homeowner already controls; both practices limit the volume of production.

Access to building materials is a serious problem in several countries. Typically, distribution is through a SOE that still enjoys a monopoly. State building companies receive a clear priority; private contractors receive materials on an "as available" basis and must resort to the black market for many items. In Hungary and Poland, however, private channels for distribution of materials have been established and most materials can be found. Nevertheless, private contractors still often pay higher prices than their SOE counterparts. Governments are confronted with the task of increasing competition by opening up more distribution channels and insuring that materials producers sell to all distributors at the same price.

Self-help Developers

Comprehensive information on the amount of production being done on a self-help basis is not available. Still, references in publications to "informal housing" production are frequent, and in Hungary, where the data are somewhat better than elsewhere, self-help housing appears in 1990 to be accounting for almost half of all production. Even in major urban areas it is an important source of production, and savings in the delivered cost of a unit are reportedly on the order of 50 percent. It is likely that Hungary represents an extreme example, but self-help production is a phenomenon that clearly deserves greater attention.

The prevalence of such production signals various forms of market inefficiency. It certainly suggests imperfections in the labor market. First, workers at over-staffed firms are very likely stealing time to work on their houses during the three- to four-year period typically required to build the unit. In a more competitive environment, they would spend the full number of hours at the job for which they are being paid. Second, to the extent that those building their units want to work more, in an efficiently operating labor market they would be able to sell these services; since those building their units are often white collar workers, including engineers, their hourly wage in their chosen profession would presumably be higher than their implied wage in house construction. Self-help building further suggests imperfections in financial markets, in which the volume of mortgage lending is restricted and/or the instruments in use are not sufficiently innovative. Finally, it probably also indicates lack of responsiveness to consumer preferences by housing developers (mostly SOEs)--such that the only way to get the type of single family unit preferred is for the household to develop it for itself, either directly through self-help or by hiring a contractor.

No policy response is needed to the problem of self-help housing. In the short term it offers a critical safety valve for satisfying consumer demand. In the longer term it should decline in importance without policy intervention as various markets become more efficient.

The Supply of Serviced Sites

Of all aspects of housing production, our information on land development is the least complete. Most fundamentally, ownership of land parcels is often unclear. To address this issue Poland, for example, is conducting a comprehensive land inventory to ascertain ownership. Other countries will also have to sort through parcel ownership. In this context a modified form of the title insurance employed in the United States might be extremely useful in permitting land development to proceed without undue delays.

As noted, the zoning and servicing of residential land in Eastern Europe over the past 40 years has been geared to providing very large sites on which SOEs developed enormous housing projects, under the conviction that their industrialized techniques could be most effectively exploited on such sites. Local governments had a relatively mechanistic role in providing buildable sites to the specifications of the SOEs.

Today the trend is for local governments to be made responsible for land development as part of the pervasive move toward decentralization of governance and fiscal responsibility. They face a sobering challenge in shifting from the "massive site" orientation required when housing production was dominated by SOEs to one consistent with smaller, possibly much smaller, scale development. The zoning process in which large blocks of land were designated for future residential development and all transactions involving individual parcels frozen will be subject to wholesale revision.[6] There will be the temptation to follow some Polish cities in adopting large lot zoning, which permits use of septic tanks and thus lowers the city's infrastructure investment costs in the short run. However, in the long run it raises the ultimate cost of providing full infrastructure services. New land use regulations should be tested against what they imply for the affordability of housing with complete services to moderate income families. "High density-low rise" residential projects are an option to be explored.

Land titling procedures in many cases will have to be simplified and rationalized. The financing of headworks (i.e., water and sewage treatment plants) and primary distribution networks (i.e., "trunk" infrastructure), previously a responsibility of central government, will have to be addressed, through development fees, higher property taxes, and bond financing.

Finally, attention must be given to helping land markets work more efficiently. Of the key ingredients for efficient markets--good information and numerous buyers and sellers--improving the flow of information is likely to need direct assistance. In some countries, for example, a citizen cannot obtain information on land transactions even if he makes a formal request at the land registrar's office. Needless to say, under such conditions widespread information on sales is not available. Buyers and sellers must invest a great deal of time in trying to assemble information from informal sources to insure that they are not paying or receiving a price badly out of line with the prevailing market. Obviously, with transactions costs so high, many potential market participants will be discouraged from participating and competition is further eroded. This situation has been offset to some degree by the emergence of private information services. The best developed brokerage market appears to be in Hungary; in Budapest a weekly real estate magazine is published which includes citations on asking prices for many parcels and units. But information on actual sales remains sparse. Opening up the flow of information is clearly within the regulatory powers of the governments concerned, and they should be strongly encouraged to do so. Once the information can be accessed, it is very likely that the private sector will perform the essential dissemination function.

STATE RENTAL HOUSING

Reform of the state rental sector is fundamental to the transformation of the housing sector. The share of all housing units accounted for the sector varies considerably among the countries discussed in this paper--ranging from 15-20 percent in Yugoslavia, Bulgaria, and Hungary, to 50 percent in Czechoslovakia.[7] In all these countries, though, a much larger share of units in urban areas are state rentals. Shifting state rentals to a market basis is essential to the development of a broader rental sector and involves the following tasks:

- Raising rents to market levels, and using the market to allocate units among households;

- Dealing with the array of property rights that occupants have established;

- Selling some rental units to their occupants or others, and selling whole projects to investors;

- Arranging financing for those who wish to purchase units; and,

- Improving the management of the remaining rental properties.

Selling State Rentals

Motivated principally by the desire to shed the responsibility for maintaining rental units, Hungary and Poland have been anxious to sell units from the state rental inventory. Several observers of developments in Eastern Europe have seen this type of "privatization" as the best way to deal with this inventory. Still many questions remain as to whether this is the best course. Indeed, Hungary, by selling units for 15 percent of their market value on an installment basis charging 3 percent interest, has sold units on terms so favorable to the purchaser that the state has actually sustained losses.

Many of the issues that arise in determining the conditions under which to sell housing units parallel those confronted in selling SOEs. Most obviously, the housing stock, like the stock of industrial assets, is extremely valuable and represents a major resource under control of the state. In Hungary, for example, the state rental stock is valued at more than the combined assets of the three largest commercial banks. These assets are so valuable that if sold at or near full value, they could provide the state with substantial funds to help during the economic transition. Difficult issues arise as to who owns the state rental stock and what rights sitting tenants have, however. Moreover, if units are sold for less than their market value, the critical issue of the distribution of the benefits between the purchaser and the state, i.e., the balance of taxpayers, arises.

Because private rental housing was not permitted in Eastern European countries (except Yugoslavia) or permitted on a very limited basis (e.g., Bulgaria), the state rental units constitute virtually the entire rental housing stock. Success in selling all of these units would mean the elimination of rental housing. Obviously, a rental sector is needed--to provide housing for newly forming families, to permit geographic mobility and other reasons. Hence, the broad privatization objective must be refined to be realistic.

In general, the opportunity to purchase a unit will be more attractive under the following conditions:

- The higher the rents charged for the unit;

- The better its condition;

- The more favorable the purchase price and financing terms;

- The weaker the protections afforded to sitting tenants.

The incentives to purchase have not been great for several reasons. First, in Eastern European countries, tenant protections are strong. Indeed, in several, occupants have formal rights of occupancy by virtue of having paid "key money" for the units; usually these rights can be inherited, and in some cases they can be sold to others with at least implicit government sanction. With strong protections, the additional comfort provided by formal ownership is modest. Second, rents have typically been very low, equivalent to only a few percent of household income. (Romania is a notable exception to this rule, where rents in state units are reported to be about half of their market levels.) The low rents make the capitalized value of rents low; consequently, occupants are only willing to consider purchasing a unit if it is sold at a deep discount and with attractive financing. In both Poland and Hungary deep discounts--85 to 90 percent of the market value--are the rule; and even then sales have been sluggish. Third, a large share of the state rental stock suffers from considerable deferred maintenance, which strongly discourages purchase, since the new owner will have to pay for such improvements in addition to the sales price whereas if he remains a tenant the state will (eventually) pay for the maintenance.

Under these conditions, raising rents is absolutely required to make the sale of the units feasible on terms that are rational for the state to accept. Selling units for less than market value will very likely result in the best units (and largest subsidies) going to those who were favored in the communist regimes (and allocated the superior units) and will result in considerable resentment by the rest of the population. The increases required to bring rents to market levels will be high--probably several hundred percent. As discussed below, the greatest hardships associated with such increased can better be offset through a program of targeted subsidies rather than through across-the-board wage increases.

Note that in a system under which an occupant's claim to a unit is conditional upon his paying the rent, the value of these rights declines as rents approach true market levels. In brief, most of the "property rights" issues are likely to disappear when rents move to market levels, assuming the authorities will enforce lease provisions requiring payment of rent.[8]

Assisting the Poor, Finance, and Management

There are at least three areas in which governments will need to act to facilitate the privatization of the state rental stock. First, in raising rents--which is the sine qua non of selling units for more than "fire sale" prices--the poorest families and pensioners will have to be protected. In short, the social safety net must be extended to the housing sector, probably in the form of a well-designed housing allowance program whose benefits can be carefully focused on the poor. Such a scheme is being implemented in East Germany and is under active consideration in Hungary. In both cases pensioners and families with low earnings are the target groups.

The Hungarian scheme would require beneficiaries to contribute a significant share of their incomes to rents (15-20 percent); beneficiaries would receive payments based on the size of unit they need, not the unit actually occupied (i.e., a single person living in a large unit would receive a subsidy based on a smaller unit and pay the extra rent out of pocket); and subsidy amounts decline at higher income levels and beyond some point they phase out completely.[9] With increased rents, which would more than pay for all maintenance costs, government could pay for a well-targeted housing allowance and still reduce its overall subsidy payments to the sector.

Second, the housing finance system will have to able to provide financing at market rates to facilitate the purchase of units. Without the availability of financing, sales will either not take place or will only occur with large subsidies.

Third, management of the properties must be changed. Currently the state rental stock (and even most of the state's other housing stock) is managed by SOEs, each of which manages tens of thousands of units. The combination of few resources and general laxity in management has led to very low levels of maintenance and other services. Both tenants paying higher rents and owners will demand better services, and these will only be forthcoming if the property management system is transformed. Moreover, a true market in rental housing will emerge only if the big SOEs are broken up and private for-profit and non-profit entities permitted to compete for management contracts on individual buildings. Where buildings are owner-occupied, the residents can select the company; in buildings that continue to be rentals, a combination of local government and residents can make the decision. The critical point, however, is to improve the services provided so that occupants see that they are receiving additional services in exchange for greater expenditures.

* * * * * *

The foregoing makes clear the challenge facing the nations of Eastern Europe in transforming their housing sectors to work along market principles. Officials in these countries realize the formidable task ahead of them and are openly seeking advice and technical assistance, and the donor community--the World Bank, USAID, the EEC, and

Western European governments--has responded with alacrity in helping Hungary and Poland. Presumably help will soon be forthcoming to the other nations. All those working on restructuring the housing sector must remember that a minimum of several years will be required to produce the broad-based changes desired. They must also remember that reform on one front has implications elsewhere in the housing sector. Short-term movement is essential, but each reform should be based on an appreciation of what it entails for all segments of the housing market.

Notes, chapter 10

1. For an excellent analysis of this problem in Hungary see Buckley et al. (1990).

2. For a description of DIMs in the Hungarian context, see Chiquier (1990); more generally, see Buckley, Lipman, and Persaud (1989).

3. Housing cooperatives are not included as a separate category since they typically contract with other entities for actual construction. The exception appears to be Czechoslovakia where some cooperatives act act as both developer and contractor.

4. See Hinds (1990) for a thorough discussion of the issues involved in privatizing SOEs.

5. The inability to compete for state projects results from there being no competition, the competition being restricted to SOEs, or failure by the state to divide projects into components of a size manageable by any but the largest firms.

6. Land prices were often frozen at the time an area was zoned for development and the owner, usually years later, was compensated on this basis.

7. For Czechoslovakia this figure includes both units owned by local housing authorities and state-sponsored rental cooperatives.

8. For a more detailed discussion of the sale of state rental units see Katsura and Struyk (1990).

9. Details are provided in Buckley et al. (1990), Annex 2.

REFERENCES

General

Hossin, Peter (1984). *Housing in Europe.* New York: St. Martin's Press.

Buckley, R., B. Lipman, and T. Persaud (1989). *Mortgage Design Under Inflation and Real Wage Uncertainty: The Use of the Dual Indexed Instrument,* Discussion Paper INU 62. Washington, DC: The World Bank.

Dougherty, A., R. van Order, and K. Villani (1982). "Pricing Shared-Appreciation Mortgages," *Housing Finance Review,* 1, 4(October): 361-375.

The Economist (1988). "Glasnost and Unemployment," *The Economist,* 310, 7530/7531 (8 January): 18.

_____ (1989a). "Niech Zyje Wiosna: Long Live Spring," *The Economist,* 312, 7614 (12 August): 1-18 (Survey of Eastern Europe).

Europa (1989). *Europa World Year Book 1989.* London: Europa Publications.

Hegedus, J. (1987). "Reconsidering the Roles of the State and the Market in Socialist Housing Systems," *International Journal of Urban and Regional Research*, 11, 1 (March): 79-97.

Hewett, Ed A. (1989) "Economic Reform in the USSR, Eastern Europe, and China: The Politics of Economics," *American Economic Review*, 79, 2(May): 16-20.

Hinds, M. (1990). *Issues in the Introduction of Market Forces in Eastern European Socialist Economies*, Report No. IDP-0057. Washington, DC: The World Bank, Office of the Vice President, European, Middle East and North Africa Region.

International Monetary Fund (1989a). "Market-Oriented Reform in Planned Economies," Report SM/89/202, European and Asian Departments, International Monetary Fund, Washington, DC. Processed.

Katsura, H., and R. Struyk (1990). *Selling Eastern Europe's Social Housing Stock: Proceed with Caution*, Report 6062-03. Washington, DC: The Urban Institute.

Kessides, Christine, Timothy King, Mario Nuti, and Catherine Sokil, eds. (1989). *Financial Reform in Socialist Economies*, EDI Seminar Series. Washington, DC: World Bank.

Kornai, J. (1990). "The Affinity Between Ownership Forms and Coordination Mechanisms: The Common Experience of Reform in Socialist Countries," *Journal of Economic Perspectives*, 4, 3: 131-147.

Lammerskitten, P. (1990). "Housing Policy and the Housing Economy in the Federal Republic of Germany," paper prepared for the National Association of Realtors, Third International Shelter Conference, Washington, DC.

Matras, Hanna (1989a). *Structure and Performance of the Housing Sector of the Centrally Planned Economies: USSR, Hungary, Poland, GDR, and Yugoslavia*, Infrastructure and Urban Development Department Discussion Paper INU 53. Washington, DC: World Bank.

_____ (1989b). *Structure and Performance of the Housing Sector of the Centrally Planned Economies: USSR, Hungary, Poland, GDR, and Yugoslavia. Part II: Comparative Database*, Urban Development Division Working Paper No. 9. Washington, DC: World Bank.

McKenzie, J.A. (1980). "A Comprehensive Look at Shared-Appreciation Mortgages," *Federal Home Loan Bank Board Journal*, November: 11-15.

Miskiewicz, Sophia M. (1986). "Housing in Eastern Europe: A 'Social Right' Abandoned," RAD Background Report 81. Washington, DC: Radio Free Europe.

Morton, Henry W. (1979). "Housing Problems and Policies of Eastern Europe and the Soviet Union," *Studies in Comparative Communism*, 12, 4(Winter): 300-321.

Sachs, Jeffrey (1990). "Eastern Europe's Economies: What is to be done?" *The Economist*, 314, 7637(13 January): 21-26.

Do I have this?

Stahl, K., and R. Struyk (1985). *U.S. and West Germany Housing Markets.* Washington, DC: The Urban Institute Press.

Struyk, Raymond J., and Mark Friedman (1989). *The Impact of a Housing-Linked Contract Savings Scheme on Households' Holdings of Financial Assets in India,* Report 3641-07-2B. Washington, DC: The Urban Institute.

World Bank (1982). *World Development Report 1982.* New York: Oxford University Press.

_____ (1989a). *World Tables: 1988-89 Edition.* Baltimore: Johns Hopkins University Press.

United Nations (1986). *World Population Prospects: Estimates and Projections as Assessed in 1984.* New York: United Nations.

_____ (1988). *Housing and Economic Adjustment.* New York: United Nations.

_____ (1989a). *Annual Bulletin of Housing and Building Statistics for Europe, 1988,* Volume 32. New York: United Nations.

_____ (1989b). *National Accounts Statistics: Main Aggregates and Detailed Tables, 1986.* New York: United Nations.

Chapter 4 - Hungary

Antal, Lazlo, and Gyorgy Suranyi (1987). "The Prehistory of the Reform of Hungary's Banking System," *Acta Oeconomica,* 38, 1-2: 35-48.

Bacskai, Tamas (1987). "The Reorganization of the Banking System," *New Hungarian Quarterly*, 28, 107 (Autumn): 127-136.

Baross, Paul (1987). "Managing the Housing Queue in Hungary," *Habitat International*, 11, 2(February): 161-175.

Bokros, L. (1987). "Conditions of the Development of Businesslike Behavior in a Two-Tier Banking System: An "Ex Ante" Evaluation of the Hungarian Banking Reform," *Acta Oeconomica*, 38, 1-2: 49-60.

Buckley, R., L. Chiquier, D. Diamond, and R. Struyk (1990). "Housing Sector Reform in Hungary." Washington, DC: The World Bank. Processed.

Chiquier, L. (1990). "Mortgage Design in Hungary." Washington, DC: The World Bank. Processed.

Creditanstalt-Bankverein (1989). "Joint Ventures in Hungary: Regulations, Current State, and Development," *CA Quarterly*, 3:39-46.

Daniel, Zsuzsa (1983). "Public Housing, Personal Income, and Central Redistribution in Hungary," *Acta Oeconomica*, 31, 1-2: 87-104.

_____ (1985). "The Effect of Housing Allocation on Social Inequality in Hungary," *Journal of Comparative Economics*, 9, 4(December): 391-409.

Daniel, Zsuzsa, and Gyula Partos (1989). "The History of the Hungarian Housing Reform: Current Issues and Lessons Learned," paper presented at Beijing, China, August 29-31.

Daniel, Zsuzsa, and Andras Semjen (1987). "Housing Shortage and Rents: The Hungarian Experience," *Economics of Planning*, 21, 1 (March): 13-29.

Economist Intelligence Unit (1989a). *Hungary: Country Profile 1989-90*. London: EIU.

Elwan, Ann (1990). Interview with Pamela Hussey. Washington, DC, February 9.

Friedlander, Michael (1988). "Hungary's Banking Reform," *Forschungsberichte Report No. 144*. Vienna: Vienna Institute for Comparative Economic Studies.

Galasi, P., and Gy. Sziratzky (1985). *Market and Second Economy in Hungary*. Frankfurt: Campus Verlag.

Hegedus, J. (forthcoming) "Self-Help Housing in Hungary," *Trialog*, 1, 8.

Hegedus, J., and I. Tosics (1983). "Housing Classes and Housing Policy: Some Changes in the Budapest Housing Market," *International Journal of Urban and Regional Research*, 7, 4(December): 467-494.

_____ (1990). "The Hungarian State-Rental Sector: Its Development and Present Problems," Budapest: Metropolitan Research Institute.

Hustzi, E. (1981). "Main Trends in the Development of Socialist Banking Systems and Organization: Relations Between Functions of Issuing (Central) Banks and Credit Banks," *Acta Oeconomica*, 26, 1-2:71-91.

International Monetary Fund (1989b). "Economic Reform in Hungary Since 1968," Report SM/89/203. European Department, International Monetary Fund, Washington, DC. Processed.

Kessides, C. (1990). "Hungary: Reform of Social Policy and Distribution System--Issues Paper." Washington, DC: The World Bank. Processed.

Komaromi, D. (1990). Interview by Pamela Hussey. Washington, DC, February 15.

Kornai, Janos (1986). "The Hungarian Reform Process: Visions, Hope, and Reality," *Journal of Economic Literature*, 24, 4(December): 1687-1737.

Martonyi, Janos (1987). "The Legal Framework for Joint Ventures in Hungary," CTC Reporter, 23(Spring): 52-53.

Ministry of Finance (1983). *Financial Conditions of Housing*. Budapest: Secretariat of the Ministry of Finance, Hungary.

Ministry of Interior (1989). *Housing Situation in Hungary*. Budapest: Department of Housing and Settlement Management.

National Bank of Hungary (1988). "Banking Developments in Hungary," *World of Banking*, 7, 4(July-August): 12-13.

Parry, David (1989). "Hungary's Changing Housing Finance System," *Housing Finance International*, 4, 2 (November): 4-12.

Schermerhorn, Jr., John R. (1990). "Report on Proposed Organization, Structure, and Staffing of the [National Property] Agency," Center for Privatization, Washington, DC. Processed.

Sillince, John A.A. (1985). "National Housing Policy in Hungary: 1945-83," *Urban Analysis*, 2(June): 243-272.

Thomas, Scott (1989). "Hungarian Economic Reform Program," USAID memorandum. Processed.

Tomlinson, Alexander C. (1990). "Report on Planning for the Establishment and Operation of the [National Property] Agency," Center for Privatization, Washington, DC. Processed.

Tosics, Ivan (1987). "Privatization in Housing Policy: The Case of Western Countries and that of Hungary," *International Journal of Urban and Regional Research*, 11, 1 (March): 61-70.

U.S. Department of Commerce (1990). Interview by Timothy Alexander with Russell Johnson, Hungary Desk Officer. Washington, DC, February 13.

Winchester, Robin (1990). Interview by Raymond Struyk. Washington, DC, February 8.

World Bank (1985). *Hungary: Investment Issues and Options*. Washington, DC: World Bank.

_____ (1989b). "Hungary: Housing Finance and Development," Infrastructure and Urban Development Department, Urban Development Division, World Bank, Washington, DC. Processed.

_____ (1989c). "Hungary: Note on the Construction Sector," Europe, Middle East, and North Africa, Technical Department, Infrastructure Division, World Bank, Washington, DC. Processed.

Wright, J. (1990). "Hungary: Housing Finance and Development Study." Washington, DC: World Bank, Infrastructure Division, Technical Department, Europe. Processed.

Chapter 5 - Poland

Carr, Josephine (1989). "Buying the Lenin-Gdansk Shipyard," *International Financial Law Review*, 9, 72 (December): 6-8.

Ciechocinska, Maria (1987). "Government Interventions to Balance Housing Supply and Urban Population Growth: The Case of Warsaw," *International Journal of Urban and Regional Research*, 11, 1(March): 9-26.

Congressional Research Service (1989). *Poland's Roundtable and U.S. Options*, Senate Print 101-39, prepared for the Committee on Foreign Relations, United States Senate. Washington, DC: Government Printing Office.

The Economist (1989b). "Big Bang, Big Adventure," *The Economist*, 313, 7634-5 (23 December): 57-58.

Economist Intelligence Unit (1989b). *Poland: Country Profile 1989-90*. London: EIU.

Frenzen, R. (1990). "Housing Cooperatives in Poland," report prepared for the Office of Housing and Urban

Programs, USAID. Washington, DC: International City Managers Association. Processed.

Government of Poland (1989). "Memorandum of Economic Policies," attachment to IMF Letter of Intent, December 22, 1989, Warsaw, Poland. Processed.

International Monetary Fund (1989c). "Economic Reform in Poland Since 1981," Report SM/89/204. European Department, International Monetary Fund, Washington, DC. Processed.

_____ (1990). "Staff Report for the 1989 Article IV Consultation and Request for Stand-By Arrangement," Report EBS/90/11. European Department and Trade Relations Department, International Monetary Fund, Washington, DC. Processed.

Kazmierczak, Andrzej (1988). "Viewing the Polish Banking System Today," *World of Banking*, 7, 4(July-August): 8-11.

Mayo, Stephen K., and James I. Stein (1988). *Housing and Labor Market Distortions in Poland: Linkages and Policy Implications*, Infrastructure and Urban Development Department Discussion Paper INU 25. Washington, DC: World Bank.

Ministry of Construction, Physical Planning, and Municipal Economy (1987). *Human Settlements Situations and Related Trends and Policies in Poland: 1981-85*, National Monograph prepared for the United Nations Economic Commission for Europe. Warsaw: Ministry of Construction, Poland.

Smith, Timothy J. (1990). "Assisting Small Enterprise Development in Poland," report prepared for the Peace Corps. Processed.

World Bank (1987). *Poland: Reform, Adjustment, and Growth (Volumes I and II)*. Washington, DC: World Bank.

_____ (1989d). "Poland: Measures to Enhance Supply Response." Photocopy.

_____ (1990). "Poland: Aide Memoire," prepared for housing sector pre-identification mission, 8-19 January. Processed.

Chapter 6 - Czechoslovakia

Blaha, Jaroslav (1984). "Le Logement en Tchecoslovakie," *Le Courrier des Pays de l'Est*, 280 (January): 38-50.

ECE Committee on Housing, Building, and Planning (1987). *Country Monograph of the Czechoslovak Socialist Republic*. Prague: United Nations Economic Commission for Europe.

Economist Intelligence Unit (1989c). *Czechoslovakia: Country Profile 1989-90*. London: EIU.

_____ (1990a). *Czechoslovakia: Country Report, No. 1*. London: EIU.

_____ (1990b). *Czechoslovakia: Country Report, No. 2*. London: EIU.

Pisova, Eva (1990). "Problems of Housing in Czechoslovakia in the Period of Transition to the Market Economy," paper presented at the World Bank Policy and Research Seminar on Housing Reforms in Socialist Economies, June, Washington, DC.

Chapter 7 - Yugoslavia

Economist Intelligence Unit (1989d). *Yugoslavia: Country Profile 1989-90.* London: EIU.

_____ (1990c). *Yugoslavia: Country Report, No. 1, 1990.* London: EIU.

_____ (1990d). *Yugoslavia: Country Report, No. 2, 1990.* London: EIU.

Flaherty, Diane (1988). "Plan, Market, and Unequal Regional Development in Yugoslavia," *Soviet Studies,* 40, 1 (January): 100-124.

Forman, Craig (1990). "Yugoslavia's Problems Show Risks in Reform of Socialist Systems," *Wall Street Journal,* 140, 35(February 20): 1,20.

Golijanin, Milan (1984). "Commercial Banks," *Yugoslav Survey,* 25, 2: 77-94.

Jeerkic, M., et al. (1988). *The Socialist Federal Republic of Yugoslavia: Monograph: 1988: Human Settlements Situation, Trends and Policies,* monograph prepared for the Committee on Housing, Building and Planning of the United Nations Economic Commission for Europe.

Murphy, Paul (1988). "The Great Debate," *The Banker*, 138 (May): 114-117.

Popovic, Bozidar (1988). "The Housing Policy and Housing," *Yugoslav Survey*, 29, 3: 99-118.

Simoneti, Marko (1990). "Housing Reform as an Integral Part of Economic Reform in Yugoslavia," paper prepared for the World Bank Seminar on Housing Reforms in Socialist Economies, June, Washington, DC.

Stefanovic, Dusan (1984). "Towns and Urban Population," *Yugoslav Survey*, 25, 2: 3-16.

Vilogorac, J., et al. (1990). "The Housing Market and Housing Finance in Yugoslavia," *Housing Finance International*, 4, 7(August).

Yugoslav Survey (1988). "Rates of Employment and Unemployment, 1980-1987," *Yugoslav Survey*, 29, 4: 27-42.

Chapter 8 - Bulgaria

Debroy, B. (1984). "Earnings, Incomes, and Living Standards in Bulgaria," *Artha Vijnana*, 26, 4 (December): 341-368.

Economist Intelligence Unit (1989e). *Bulgaria: Country Profile 1989*. London: EIU.

_____ (1990e). *Romania, Bulgaria, Albania: Country Report*, No. 1. London: EIU.

Galavanakov, K. (1990). "New Legislature Opens Up Bulgarian Economy." Processed.

Ganev, Christo (1989). "The Urban Process and the Appearance of Agglomerations in Bulgaria," *Socio-Economic Planning Science*, 23, 1/2: 17-22.

Grigorov, N., et al. (1987). *Human Settlements Situation: Trends and Policies in Bulgaria: National Monograph*, prepared for the People's Republic of Bulgaria, Committee for Regional and Urban Planning, Council of Ministers. Sofia: UN Economic Commission for Europe.

Kolvea, M., and M. Giorov (1990). "Bulgaria," in *Housing Finance in Eastern Europe: Proceedings of a Conference in Budapest*, 14-16 June 1990, Mark Boleat (ed.). International Union of Housing Finance Institutions: Chicago.

McIntyre, Robert J. (1988). *Bulgaria: Politics, Economics, and Society*. New York: Pinter.

Parry, David L., Maya T. Koleva, and Evgeni M. Popov (1990). "Bulgarian *Housing Markets and Mortgage Financing,*" *Housing Finance International*. 4, 4 (May): 27-30.

Petkov, Tsvetan (1990). "Benefits to Invest in Bulgaria." Processed.

Petkov, K.L., and J.E.M. Thirkell (1988). "Managerial Elections in Bulgaria: Conflicts and Representation," *Labour and Society*, 13, 3 (July): 285-298.

Tabakov, Todor (1990). "Legal Procedures for Setting Up Joint Operations or Foreign Subsidiaries: Priority Sectors of Development, Investment Leads." Processed.

Walliamann, Isidor, and Christo Stojanov (1989). "Social and Economic Reform in Bulgaria: Economic Democracy and Problems of Change in Industrial Relations," *Economic and Industrial Democracy: An International Journal*, 10 (August): 361-378.

Chapter 9 - Romania

Crowther, William E. (1988). *The Political Economy of Romanian Socialism*. New York: Praeger.

Daniel, Odile (1983). "Les Politiques du Logement en Hongrie et en Romanie," *Le Courrier des Pays de l'Est*, 274 (June): 34-49.

Dorin, Aldea (1990). "Some Economic and Legal Considerations upon House-Building Financing in Romania," paper presented at the World Bank Policy and Research Seminar on Housing reforms in Socialist Economies, June, Washington, DC.

East European Markets (1990). "More Hard Currency Needed," *East European Markets*, 10, 12 (June 15): 12.

Economist Intelligence Unit (1989f). *Romania: Country Profile 1989*. London: EIU.

_____ (1990e). *Romania, Bulgaria, Albania: Country Report*, No. 1. London: EIU.

Gilberg, Trond (1990). *Nationalism and Communism in Romania: The Rise and Fall of Ceausescu's Personal Dictatorship*. Boulder: Westview Press.

Hunya, Gabor (1989). "Village Systemisation in Romania: Historical, Economic, and Ideological Background," *Communist Economics*, 1, 3: 327-341.

Nankman, Piet (1990). "Housing in Romania." Processed.